Bilingualism as Interactional Practices

Bilingualism as Interactional Practices

Joseph Gafaranga

EDINBURGH
University Press

Edinburgh University Press is one of the leading university
presses in the UK. We publish academic books and journals
in our selected subject areas across the humanities and social
sciences, combining cutting-edge scholarship with high
editorial and production values to produce academic works
of lasting importance. For more information visit our website:
edinburghuniversitypress.com

Edinburgh University Press Ltd
The Tun – Holyrood Road
12(2f) Jackson's Entry
Edinburgh EH8 8PJ

Typeset in 10.5/12 pt Janson MT
by Servis Filmsetting Ltd, and
printed and bound in Great Britain by
CPI Group (UK) Ltd, Croydon CR0 4YY

A CIP record for this book is available from the British
Library

ISBN 978 0 7486 7595 1 (hardback)
ISBN 978 0 7486 7596 8 (webready PDF)
ISBN 978 0 7486 7598 2 (epub)

Contents

List of illustrations

Acknowledgements

This book about bilingual interaction is itself a result of countless inter-actions I have had with so many people over so many years that it would take another book to list them all, even if that were possible. Going back twenty years, I owe a debt of gratitude to my mentors and supervi-sors at Lancaster University, notably Professor Marilyn Martin Jones and Dr Mark Sebba, and, through them, to the Bilingualism Research Group as a whole. Contemporary members of the group I cannot fail to mention include Maria Carme Torras, Eva Codó and Katherine Jones. During those years at Lancaster University, I got to talk to some all-time authorities in the field of bilingualism, including Professor Peter Auer, Professor Li Wei, Professor Monica Heller, Professor Carole Myers-Scotton and others. I am forever grateful for your time. But I also have to acknowledge the, at that time, less established scholars such as Peter Martin (RIP), Jo Shoba, Melissa Moyer and others I conversed with at the margins of conferences.

Post Lancaster, I had significant interactions with members of the Concordance Group at the GKT School of Medicine (King's College London), notably Professor Nicky Britten and her team. I am so grateful to them all for introducing me to the fascinating world of doctor–patient interaction and indeed for giving me access to the data they had col-lected before I joined them. As a member of this group, I had the unique opportunity to meet and talk to conversation analysts such as Professor Paul Drew, Professor John Heritage, Professor Paul Seedhouse, amongst others. These interactions led to an increased interest in conversation analysis and to the urge for a connection between my background in bilingualism studies and the study of social interaction in general. Without doubt, this urge will be felt in the pages of this book.

In October 2002, I joined the University of Edinburgh as a lecturer in Discourse Analysis and I have taught courses in this area ever since. But I also took the first opportunity to introduce courses in the area of the sociolinguistics of bilingualism. This book therefore is also a result of the interactions I have had over those years with students and colleagues at the University of Edinburgh. The Language in Context Research Group, its founding members Professor John Joseph and Professor Mariam Meyerhoff in particular, are acknowledged. I also acknowledge the many students, both undergraduate and postgraduate, who have taken my courses and those whose honours and MSc dissertations I have supervised. I am particularly grateful to Dr Florence Bonacina-Pugh and Dr Ifigenia Papagergiou, who, as PhD students, have spent a good part of their lives thinking and writing about bilingualism with me.

This book would not have been written without the generosity of the various institutions and organisations that have supported my research over the years. These include the Pilkington Charitable Trust, Lancaster University, Centre for the Assistance of Refugee Academics (CARA), University of Edinburgh, Art and Humanities Research Council (AHRC), Economic and Social Research Council (ESRC), British Academy (BA), Nuffield Foundation, and so on. They are all acknowledged here. Also acknowledged are the many people whose interactions I have analysed, notably members of the Rwandan community in Belgium and the various contributors to the online newspaper www.igihe.com. I am grateful to publishers Palgrave Macmillan, Cambridge University Press, Sage Publications and Mouton de Gruyter, not only for publishing the original papers the chapters of this book are based on, but also for allowing me to rework and re-use them for the purpose of this book. And I am grateful to the anonymous reviewers for their contribution to the quality of those papers and, by implication, of the chapters of this book.

Last but not least, as always, I am grateful to my family, immediate and extended, for a safe, welcoming and comfortable social environment without which the simplest act, let alone writing a book, would have been unbearable.

Transcription conventions

The following are some of the conventions used in data transcripts. Otherwise, refer to original source:

Language contrast	Kinyarwanda
	French
	<u>*Other language*</u>
(.)	Pause (with or without measured length)
[	Overlapping talk
((laughter))	Non-verbal action
(unclear)	With or without transcriber's best guess
Bold	Target element
Saucissons- yewe waje	Recycle / restart
{first name}	Name omitted

Free English translation in a separate sequence after the original. Letters of the alphabet (A, B, C, etc.) are used for participants so as to preserve their anonymity; where appropriate, P, D and Ch specifically represent 'patient', 'doctor' and 'child', respectively.

1 Introduction

1.1 Where it all started

The Kinyarwanda expression 'Kuvuga indimi ebyiri' literally means 'to speak two languages', i.e. to be bilingual. However, the expression can also be used non-literally and mean either 'to say one thing and mean another' or 'to say one thing to one person and another to another person'. That is to say, when used non-literally, the expression evokes less than positive connotations for the person described as speaking 'indimi ebyiri' (two languages). Whether Rwandans actually associate bilingualism with negative connotations is an empirical question I prefer to leave alone for the moment. However, it is worth noting that such negative attitudes towards bilingualism have been documented in other contexts. A Cambridge University professor is reported to have said:

> If it were possible for a child to live in two languages at once equally well, so much the worse. His intellectual and spiritual growth would not thereby be doubled, but halved. Unity of mind and character would have great difficulty in asserting itself in such circumstances. (Laurie, 1890: 15)

In educational contexts, bilingual children were, until recently, categorised as having 'special needs', with all the negative connotations that this entails. As a result, special provisions (often less than ideal) were made available to help them shed their bilingualism and become monolingual. Certainly, the fact that the children concerned had access to two or more languages was not celebrated as such. The children's bilingualism, rather than monolingual teaching and assessment, was blamed for their apparently unsatisfactory school performance. At the level of the wider community, the monolingual ideology, and the resulting stigmatisation of bilingualism, show in the idealised notion of 'monolingual state'. The slogan 'one nation, one language' remains, to this date, such a powerful one that states that are actually multilingual adopt monolingual

1

policies. The view is held that bilingualism is a threat to national unity, and therefore a bad thing. The following comment (Marten and Kula, 2008: 306) refers to post-independence Zambia but could apply to many other contexts, African and non-African, with only slight modification:

> tribalism and centrifugal tendencies were seen as a threat to the new country and the establishment of 'national identity' became a paramount task: the national motto adopted after independence was 'One Zambia, One Nation'. It is against this background that English became the national and official language of Zambia, which was based on the view that English would help integrate the different Zambian peoples, while African languages were seen as promoting factionism and tribalism. 'One Zambia, One Nation, One Language' could thus have been the appropriate extension of the national motto at the time.

Along the same lines, President Roosevelt is reported to have said in 1917:

> We must have but one flag. We must also have but one language. That language must be the language of the Declaration of Independence, of Washington's Farewell address, of Lincoln's Gettysburg speech and second inaugural . . . We call upon all loyal and unadulterated Americans to man the trenches against the enemy within our gates. (cited in Crawford, 1992: 85)

More recently, and on European soil, the French Constitutional Council objected to the ratification of the European Charter for Regional and Minority Languages on the grounds that it violated the constitutional principles of the indivisibility of the Republic, equality before the law and unicity of the French people (Montvalon, 2015). Of course, the monolingual ideology, as any other ideology, need not be so explicitly stated; often it has to be deduced from actual practices.

Negative attitudes have also been directed towards bilingual language use, also known as code-switching (CS).[1] The alternate use of two or more languages within the same interaction has often been seen as resulting from the speakers' laziness and lack of attention, and, worst of all, as reflecting the speakers' deficient mastery of the languages involved. The reasoning went: if one were able to carry out a conversation in one or the other of the two languages, there would not be any reason to use both concurrently. An example of such negative attitudes towards bilingual language use is the following statement by a Rwandan 'linguist':

> For us, French is the French language, vehicle of the French culture and its Belgian and Canadian counterparts. Kinyarwanda is a Bantu language,

vehicle of the Rwandan culture. Diluted French, whether it is called 'Rwandisme' or any other 'Africanisme', conjures in us a feeling of repulsion. The same feeling is experienced in relation to diluted Kinyarwanda that some are already calling 'Ikinyafaransa' and which consists of a rude mixture and inappropriate borrowings. (Gasana, 1984: 224; my translation from French)

Today, however, the situation seems to have improved and CS 'is gradually gaining acceptability' (Gardner-Chloros, 2009: 82). One reason for this improvement, according to Gardner-Chloros, is the general trend towards greater tolerance of 'cultural, racial, musical, culinary and other types of hybridity' in today's society (Gardner-Chloros, 2009: 82). Concurrently with these sociocultural developments, a great deal of research has been undertaken since the last quarter of the twentieth century that questioned the previously held beliefs. Elsewhere, I have referred to this body of research as a rehabilitation effort (Gafaranga, 2007a; also see Chapter 2 in this book). Thus, today, bilingualism is reported to have communicative, cultural and cognitive advantages (Baker and Prys Jones, 1998; Wei, 2000; Chin and Wigglesworth, 2007, etc.) and CS is, contrary to previous beliefs, said to reflect speakers' high competence in the languages involved. Statements such as the following from Poplack (1980 / 2000: 2260–1) are not uncommon in the CS literature:

These findings (...) provide strong evidence that code-switching is a verbal skill requiring a large degree of linguistic competence in more than one language, rather than a defect arising from insufficient knowledge of one or the other.

The rehabilitation of bilingualism and bilingual language use has been so deep that, nowadays, less than full competence in all of one's languages is no longer seen as something to be ashamed about. Rather there is an increased recognition that linguistic competence is situated and varies from speaker to speaker according to their communicative needs, and that the languages in one's repertoire are resources available to be drawn on for specific interactional purposes. Thus new terms such as 'plurilingual competence', 'translanguaging', 'metrolingualism' and so on are emerging, each one recognising this new conceptual reality.

1.2   Researching bilingualism as interactional practices

With the rehabilitation of bilingualism comes a different issue, namely that of 'where to from here?'. In the case of language alternation studies, this rehabilitation raises the issue of their future direction, nature and purpose. In a paper on 'the rationality of reading activities', the ethnomethodologist James Heap (1990) makes some interesting statements about scholarship. Any scholarship, he says, 'aims to deliver "news"'. In turn, deliverable news is either critical or positive. Critical news is usually of the type 'things are not as they appear,' but it may also be of the type 'others have got it wrong as to how things are.' As for positive news, it usually is of the type 'X is organised this way' (1990: 42). Interestingly, with specific reference to ethnomethodology, Heap remarks that critical news is associated with early ethnomethodology while positive news is associated with current developments in the field (1990: 42). Finally, Heap notes that, for any domain of enquiry to continue to be interesting, 'a critical news approach, at some juncture, must develop ways of, and interests in, delivering some positive news' (1990: 43).

Heap's views apply very well to the case of research in bilingualism, and to bilingual interaction in particular. Mainstream CS research so far has clearly been geared towards delivering critical news. The meta-statement has been that bilingual language use 'is not as it appears', that those who see it as random 'have got it wrong' (Heap, 1990: 42). For example, while CS was previously viewed, as we have seen, as reflecting speakers' lack of competence in the languages involved, researchers have gone on to claim that CS is actually an indication of the user's advanced mastery of the languages in contact. Indeed, advanced mastery of the languages involved has come to be assumed to be the starting point. As Meeuwis and Blommaert (1998: 77) note, one of the foundational assumptions in CS research is that 'the languages are (. . .) available and accessible to the speakers in (the) particular society (under investigation), and that *the code-switching speakers actually "know" the languages* (my italics).' However, even as the myth of lack of competence as the reason for CS was dispelled, the question of why people who know two languages would use them concurrently in the same conversation remained and researchers addressed it by arguing that CS is functional, hence the various functional models of CS (see Chapter 2). That is to say, the rehabilitation of CS has been undertaken within the confines of the prevailing ideology. Therefore, because the negative news has largely been delivered, the time has come for bilingualism research, and research in bilingual interaction in particular, to begin to deliver 'positive news if it is to keep its audience' (Heap, 1990: 43).

How might the study of bilingualism, and of bilingual language use in particular, proceed so as to deliver positive news? CS research is very diverse in terms of researchers' backgrounds and interests, such that it is not possible to predict exactly what directions the various interests will take. One interesting area of CS research, which will be the focus of this book, is known as the *'organisational'* perspective (Sebba and Wootton, 1998; Gafaranga, 2007a). In this perspective, the negative news statement is that language alternation is not random because it contributes to the organisation of the interaction in which it occurs. Auer, who is the uncontested pioneer of this perspective, puts its essence as in the following:

> In the organization of bilingual conversation, participants face two types of tasks. First, there are problems specifically addressed to language choice (. . .). Second, participants have to solve a number of problems related to the organization of conversation in general, e.g. turn-taking, topic cohesions, (. . .) the constitution of specific linguistic activities. *The alternating use of two languages may be a means of coping with these problems.* (1988 / 2000: 170; my emphasis)

Indeed, CS has been observed to coincide with such significant interactional aspects of talk organisation such as turn-taking, repair, sequence organisation and so on. However, the question of exactly how the contribution of CS to the organisation of the interaction in which it appears ('X is organised this way') can be accounted for is not always explicitly addressed. There is a need to go beyond merely noticing the presence of CS in specific interactional practices to actually explicating how those interactional practices that involve language alternation work. For example, CS has frequently been observed in the interactional site of direct speech reporting. However, merely noticing the presence of CS in this site is not enough. As I show in Chapter 3, a deeper understanding of the role of language choice in this site is gained if the practice of speech representation in bilingual conversation is focused on in its own right, rather than as part of a wider theory of bilingual conversation in general. The overall message of this book is that it is by focusing on specific interactional practices involving the use of two languages that the study of bilingualism, and of bilingual interaction in particular, can begin to deliver what Heap refers to as 'positive news'. In other words, the message is that, now that bilingual language use has been rehabilitated, now that the previously held negative attitudes have been dispelled, for research in bilingual interaction to continue to be interesting, researchers must turn their attention to describing in detail specific interactional practices in bilingual interaction, hence the title of this book, 'Bilingualism as Interactional Practices'.

1.3　Mainstreaming bilingualism studies

In the same paper on the 'rationality of reading activities' discussed above, Heap (1990) makes a distinction between two types of audience and, therefore, two types of research: namely, 'applied (ethnomethodology)' and 'straight-ahead (ethnomethodology)'.

> Straight-ahead EM is done for, and reported to, other professional (including students) ethnomethodologists. It provides knowledge of some state of affairs, affairs chosen for study because of their value for furthering the development of ethnomethodological knowledge. Applied EM is done for, and reported to, persons perhaps having only a nodding acquaintance with EM. The affairs studied are those whose formal structures may have consequences important to this audience of 'lay ethnomethodologists.' The affairs chosen for study have value for, and to, them. (Heap, 1990: 43–4)

A similar distinction is made by Ten Have (1999) between 'pure conversation analysis' (CA) and 'applied CA'. However, Ten Have (1999) notes that the term 'applied CA' can be used in either of two senses. On the one hand, it may be used to refer to 'CA-like practices', which address the concerns of 'various "neighbouring" disciplines such as sociology, anthropology, (social) psychology and (socio)-linguistics'; on the other, it may be used to refer to work targeted to the concerns of 'people who have a practical, moral and / or political interest in the practices studied, in terms of the situations, organizations, and / or institutions that are co-constituted by those practices' (1999: 161). Only in the latter sense are Heap and Ten Have in total agreement. Other researchers who have focused on this distinction warn against it, for it is potentially misleading. For them, the distinction between 'applied CA' and 'pure CA' is not methodological. As Richards puts it (2005: 3), applied CA is CA in the first place and, 'however we may choose to characterise (it), it must above all meet the analytically rigorous demands of all CA practice worthy of that name.'

In the area of CS research, the position has been that the CA perspective on CS is 'applied CA'. In this respect, the following statement from Wei is significant:

> The *applications of CA* to the study of bilingual interaction began against the background of quantitative analysis of grammatical patterns in bilingual data, and the macro-level sociolinguistic analysis of external factors affecting language choice. In particular, researchers tended to explain meanings of code-switching (. . .) in terms of power relations within the speech community, the symbolic values of different languages, and / or

the socio-psychological motivations of speakers. Peter Auer, one of the first researchers who *used CA* to examine bilingual interaction, questioned the way in which the meaning of code-switching was understood. (Wei, 2002: 164; my emphasis)

As this passage makes clear, work on CS was undertaken, not to do CA per se, but rather to use CA for what was believed to be a non-CA purpose. Auer himself speaks, not of doing CA, but of 'flexing the muscles of CA'. And, describing his own work, he refers to it as an 'attempt (. . .) to *apply* a CA-type approach to data in which two or more languages are used' (1998: 2). That is to say, along with Ten Have, one can speak of 'CA-like practices'.

If, as maintained in this book, bilingualism is viewed in terms of specific interactional practices, the distinction between 'applied CA' and 'pure CA' becomes obsolete. From its inception, in its broad sense, CA is understood as the study of 'conversational practices'. Naturally, as no further specification is attached, those involving bilingual language use are candidates for CA investigation. Also, in a restricted sense, CA is understood as the study of talk organisation, more precisely as the study of how conversational practices are organised. According to Psathas:

> CA studies the organization / orderliness of social action, particularly those social actions that are located in everyday interaction, in *discursive practices*, in the sayings / tellings / doings of members of society. (1995: 2; my emphasis)

In the case of bilingual interaction, a convincing case has now been made that 'language choice (is) a significant aspect of talk organisation' (Gafaranga, 1999). In other words, in investigating the organisation of interactional practices in which bilingual language use is involved, to borrow from Heap (1990), one adds to knowledge about talk organisation and, therefore, does CA. By way of an example, consider the account of repair practices in bilingual conversation, as proposed in Chapter 5. The structure of repair in conversation has already been widely studied in CA and, in investigating the practice in bilingual conversation, I add to that pre-existing knowledge. In other words, I describe language choice as a significant dimension of repair organisation. In short, the key claim in the book is that one way to ensure that the study of bilingualism, and of bilingual interaction in particular, can continue to be relevant and interesting is by mainstreaming it.

The mainstreaming of the study of bilingualism can be achieved in one or both of two ways. On the one hand, the practices to be investigated may have been described in monolingual conversation. In this case, the new research explicitly builds on the existing knowledge, which it may add to, confirm or reject. The following comment by a most authoritative scholar, although phrased with reference to the study of grammatical aspects of CS, is relevant for the study of bilingualism as interactional practices as well: 'findings about the grammatical structure of languages in contact may reinforce existing analyses of individual languages, or may even offer new insights not available when a language is studied in its own right' (Myers-Scotton, 2002: 4). To use the example of repair in bilingual conversation (Chapter 5) again, an important theoretical claim in the literature on repair in conversation is that 'nothing is, in principle, excludable from the class "repairable"' (Schegloff et al., 1977: 363). By demonstrating that language choice itself can be repaired, the chapter contributes to this theoretical position by providing further evidence of it. Alternatively, the practice to be described might be new. In this case, mainstreaming means approaching the practice with a recognisable methodology that can also be applied to the same or similar practices in monolingual interaction. In Richards's words, the practice must be approached with 'the analytically rigorous demands of all CA practice worthy of that name' (2005: 3). To give an example, Chapter 3 presents the methodology I will use in analysing bilingual practices in later chapters and illustrates it using a monolingual case.

1.4 An inductive perspective

Earlier, I indicated that the focus of this book is going to be the organisational perspective on bilingual interaction. I have also linked this perspective to CA. While CA will provide the main 'analytic mentality' (Schenkein, 1978), no orthodoxy is intended. In one of his most important contributions, Auer states the following:

> any theory of conversational code-alternation is bound to fail if it does not take into account that the meaning of code-alternation depends in essential ways on its 'sequential environment'. This is given, in the first place, by the conversational turn immediately preceding it, to which code-alternation may respond in various ways. While the preceding verbal activities provide the contextual frame for a current utterance, the following utterance by a next participant reflects his or her interpretation of that preceding utterance. Therefore, following utterances are important cues for the analyst and for the first speaker as to if and how a first utterance has been understood. (1995: 116)

In other words, Auer advocates a sequential analysis. For this reason, elsewhere (Gafaranga, 2007b) I have described Auer's approach as a 'local order' perspective, while recognising that an 'overall order' perspective on bilingual interaction is also possible. The significance of this observation is not so much that one perspective is better than the other, but rather that no one perspective can exhaust all possibilities. That is to say, sequential analysis may be appropriate for some practices and quite unfit for some others. For example, while sequential analysis might be appropriate for describing the practice of conversational repair in bilingual conversation, it certainly is not for the practice of translinguistic apposition (Chapter 6). As we will see, translinguistic apposition occurs in written discourse, and specifically in written texts addressed to a general and anonymous readership. Sebba (2013) has convincingly made the case for the inadequacy of sequential analysis for CS in written texts. Therefore, in approaching bilingualism as interactional practices, an open-mind attitude as to the appropriate approach must be adopted, allowing each observed practice and the specific questions raised about it to dictate the actual approach to adopt.

However, open-mindedness should not be equated with an 'anything goes' attitude at the level of research questions and, therefore, at the level of approaches. Wei (1998) identifies two broad questions that the study of bilingual conversation can address: namely, 'why'-questions and 'how'-questions. Why-questions lead to motivational explanations of CS. A typical example of such an explanation is Myers-Scotton's account of CS, as summarised in Chapter 2. As we will see, for Myers-Scotton, in approaching bilingual language use, the key question to ask is: 'what motivates speakers to switch languages within a single conversation?' (Myers-Scotton and Bolonyai, 2001: 6). As for how-questions, they lead to organisational explanations. Examples of how-questions are: how does this interactional practice involving language alternation work? How is this sequence involving language alternation organised? How does CS contribute to this practice? An important feature of these how-questions is that they are exploratory and do not presume a particular answer (in the form of a pre-formulated hypothesis). Rather, in order to answer these kinds of questions, data must be approached inductively. This book argues that, in order to investigate bilingualism as interactional practices, an inductive attitude must be adopted, not least because there can never be one hypothesis – that is, one theory – for all practices, some of which might not have been described before. It is hoped that the methodological proposals suggested in Chapter 3 will ensure the required analytical rigour across practices.

1.5   The book and its content

Hoey (2001) makes a distinction between two types of text: namely, mainstream texts and colony texts. According to Hoey, some of the features of a text as a colony, which differentiate it from a mainstream text, are:

1. Meaning not derived from sequence
2. Adjacent units do not form continuous prose
3. There is a framing context
4. One component may be used without referring to the others
5. Components can be reprinted or reused in subsequent works
6. Components may be added, removed or altered. (2001: Ch. 5)

Typical examples of colonies include works such as dictionaries, hymn books, academic journals and multi-authored collections.

The overall organising principle in this book is that of a text as a colony. The book consists of five content chapters, in addition to this Introduction and a Conclusion. The current Introduction and its expansion in Chapters 2 and 3, along with the Conclusion, can be seen as providing the frame uniting the illustrative case studies in Chapters 4, 5 and 6, each of which is independent of the others. Once the frame is understood, each of these case studies can be read independently. A particularly relevant feature of a text as a colony is that components can be 'reused in subsequent works'. Each of the case studies, and indeed the review in Chapter 2, has previously been published in a different version to serve a different purpose. Chapter 2 reworks a contribution made to an edited collection with the title 'Code-switching as a conversational strategy' (see Gafaranga, 2007a, in the References). Chapter 4 is based on a chapter previously included in *Talk in Two Languages* with the title 'Using the models: Direct speech reporting in talk in two languages' (see Gafaranga, 2007b, in the References). Chapter 5 adapts a journal article previously published in the *International Journal of Bilingualism* (see Gafaranga, 2012, in the References). And Chapter 6 is based on a journal article previously published in *Language in Society* with the title 'Translinguistic apposition in a multilingual media blog in Rwanda' (see Gafaranga, 2015, in the References). In this book, these various pieces of research are collected together in support of the view of bilingualism as interactional practices. As the data used and their sociolinguistic contexts have already been described in those previous publications, no need is felt here to reproduce those descriptions, except, as in the case of Chapter 6, where the practice under discussion is accounted for in terms of the very same sociolinguistic context. As will become clear, unlike the practices described in Chapters 4 and 5, the practice described in Chapter 6 is context-specific. Therefore suffice it to say that the data used in this book come from three main sources: (1) a corpus of bilingual French–Kinyarwanda conversations among Rwandans who live in Belgium; (2) a corpus of general practice consultations collected in the Midlands and South-east of England; and (3) a corpus of news articles collected from www.igihe.com, a Rwandan multilingual online media outlet. As indicated above, an important feature of a colony is that components may be added, removed or altered. Out of a potentially infinite number of bilingual practices, only three are included in this book. I would like to invite researchers to contribute to this text, i.e. to add new cases in support of the view of bilingualism as interactional practices. In turn, this is consistent with the view of CA, the mentality of which is adopted in this book, as 'an accumulation of empirical findings about (...) multiple practices organizing social action' rather than as one coherent theory (Heritage and Clayman, 2010: 14).

1.6 Summary

The study of bilingualism, and of CS in particular, has been undertaken against the background of very negative attitudes towards it. As a consequence, studies have, on the whole, been geared towards rehabilitating bilingualism and bilingual language use. From being regarded as a problem, bilingualism is currently seen, if not as an advantage, at least as a resource. Likewise, from being considered a sign of lack of competence, bilingual language use is seen as a sign of high competence in the languages involved and as serving specific interactional tasks in the interaction where it is observed. However, this rehabilitation of bilingualism raises an entirely new problem: where to from here? How can the study of bilingualism continue to be interesting and relevant? Focusing on CS and, within this, on a specific perspective on it, namely the organisational perspective, this book argues that, for studies of CS to continue to be interesting and relevant, bilingualism must be understood as consisting of diverse interactional practices. Therefore, it is argued that, moving forward, research will aim to build an ever-growing collection of detailed descriptions of interactional practices involving the use of two or more languages. The remainder of this book details the rehabilitation effort that has been undertaken to bring us where we are today, proposes a methodology that can be used in moving forward and illustrates it with three case studies, all the while inviting other researchers to contribute to this new direction.

Note

1. Many different terms are used to refer to the alternate use of two languages, including code-switching, language alternation, code-mixing, translanguaging and so on. All these terms are not necessarily equivalent and may convey different shades of meanings. In this book, for convenience, no attempt is made to keep them separate, leaving the context to disambiguate them.

2 The rehabilitation of code-switching

2.1 Introduction

As I have indicated in the previous chapter, the study of bilingual language use or CS has been undertaken against the backdrop of very negative attitudes and it is for this reason that it can be seen as a rehabilitation effort. This attempt to demonstrate that CS is not a random phenomenon has been undertaken from two main perspectives, namely a grammatical perspective and a sociofunctional perspective. On the one hand, researchers such as Poplack (1980), Sebba (1998), Myers-Scotton (1993a), Muysken (2000) and others have argued that, at the grammatical level, language alternation is very orderly, even though its orderliness may be different from that of the languages involved. On the other hand, researchers such as Gumperz (1982), Auer (1984) and Myers-Scotton (1993b) have argued that, from a sociofunctional perspective, the use of two or more languages within the same conversation serves specific interactional tasks for participants. Figure 2.1 (from Gafaranga, 2009: 119) captures these two general perspectives on the study of CS.

In this chapter, I will limit myself to the work undertaken under the sociofunctional perspective for it is most relevant for the purpose of this book. However, even here, not every piece of work undertaken under

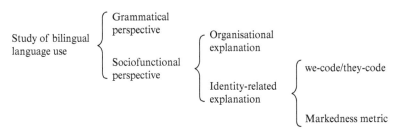

Figure 2.1   Approaches to language alternation in bilingual conversation

this perspective will be examined; rather, I will limit myself to the major landmarks.

2.2 Code-switching as a contextualisation cue

John Gumperz is credited as the uncontested pioneer of the study of CS. To be sure, Gumperz investigated CS in the context of developing a general theory of interaction known as Interactional Sociolinguistics. He stated his motivation as in the following:

> There is a need for a social theory which accounts for the communicative functions of linguistic variability and for its relation to speakers' goals without reference to untestable functionalist assumptions about conformity or non-conformance to closed systems of norms. (1982: 93)

In this programmatic statement, Gumperz positions himself relative to the two then-prevailing paradigms of work: namely, Labovian variationist sociolinguistics and Fishman's diglossia. Labov (1966) and his followers had been describing regularity in language variation by correlating language variables and social attributes such as social class, age, gender and so on. Following Ferguson (1959), Fishman (1967 / 2000), for his part, had been accounting for language variation in functional terms. He wrote:

> The use of several separate codes within a single society (and their stable maintenance rather than the displacement of one by the other over time) (is) dependent on each code serving functions distinct from those considered appropriate for the other. (Fishman, 1967 / 2000: 81)

Gumperz distanced himself from these two traditions and proposed a focus on actual face-to-face communication. As can be read in the quotation above, according to Gumperz, language varies (sociolinguistics); variation in language serves communicative functions (Fishman); but the functionality of language variation has to be examined at the level of face-to-face communication and taking into account participants' agency. According to Gumperz, 'communication is a social activity requiring the *coordinated efforts of two or more individuals*. Mere talk to produce sentences, no matter how well formed or elegant the outcome is, does not by itself constitute communication' (1982: 1; emphasis added).

Clearly, in this view of what communication is, a central issue is how this coordination is achieved and how meanings are negotiated in situ. An example of the kinds of problem Interactional Sociolinguistics should help solve is the following:

individuals who speak English well and have no difficulty in producing grammatical English sentences may nevertheless differ significantly in what they perceive as meaningful discourse cues. Accordingly, their assumption about what information is to be conveyed, how it is to be ordered and put into words and their ability to fill in the unverbalized information they need to make sense of what transpires may also vary. This may lead to misunderstandings (. . .). (Gumperz, 1982: 172)

That is to say, Interactional Sociolinguistics should account for the fact that people may fail to understand each other, even when they share a common lexico-grammatical system. Indeed, the study of (cross-cultural) (mis)communication has occupied centre-stage in Interactional Sociolinguistics. Conversely, therefore, Interactional Sociolinguistics should also explicate how participants in interaction manage to communicate successfully. According to Gumperz, both successful communication and the lack of it are a matter of *contextualisation cues*. A contextualisation cue, he writes, is any 'surface feature of message form which (. . .) speakers (use to) *signal* and listeners (to) interpret what the activity is, how semantic content is to be understood and how each sentence relates to what precedes or follows' (1982: 131; emphasis added). Such cues may be phonetic, syntactic, lexical or stylistic variables. They may consist of formulaic routines, formulaic expressions, discourse routines such as openings and closings, speech delivery features such as prosody (loudness, tempo, stress, intonation, silence, laughter, back channels) and even language alternation (Gumperz, 1982: 129). Note the parallel between Gumperz's notion of contextualisation cue and Saussure's (1959) notion of 'marginal features' of language.

How does language alternation fit into Gumperz's view of face-to-face communication? Gumperz is actually very explicit about this. CS is a type of contextualisation cue.

> Code switching signals contextual information equivalent to what in monolingual settings is conveyed through prosody or other syntactic or lexical processes. It generates the presuppositions in terms of which the content of what is said is decoded. (1982: 98)

Thus, to paraphrase Heap (1990), Gumperz's negative news statement relative to previously held assumptions about CS can be formulated. According to Gumperz, these assumptions are wrong ('things are not as they appear' / 'other people have got it wrong') because CS is a contextualisation cue.

As we have seen, to continue to be interesting, scholarship must go beyond negative news statements and offer positive news. Positive news statements are formulated along the lines of 'X is organised / works this way' (Heap, 1990). Gumperz oriented to this need for positive news by explicating how CS works as a contextualisation cue. An important aspect of contextualisation cues, according to Gumperz, is that they are conventional, and their meanings vary from culture to culture. Thus, when these cues are shared by all participants, 'interpretive processes are taken for granted and tend to go unnoticed. However, when (they are not shared), interpretation may differ and misunderstanding may occur' (1982: 132). Using this as a backdrop, Gumperz works up the conventionality of CS as a contextualisation cue, starting from a claim of division of labour between the languages in a bilingual society. He postulates the distinction *we-code / they-code*. In a bilingual community,

> The tendency is for the ethnically specific, minority language to be regarded as the 'we code' and become associated with in-group and informal activities, and for the majority language to serve as the 'they code' associated with more formal, stiffer and less personal out-group relations. (1982: 66)

Such an association between language varieties and social values comes about through frequent language use following patterns of language choice such as those described in models of diglossia (Ferguson, 1959; Fishman, 1967). On the other hand, because of this association, language varieties and situations in which they are used, identities they are associated with, and social values they communicate become co-selective. Having established this association between language varieties and social meanings, Gumperz draws the logical conclusion that CS has 'a semantic value' (1982: 93).

> The semantic effect of metaphorical code switching depends on the existence of a regular relationship between variables and social situations (. . .). The context in which one of a set of alternates is regularly used becomes part of its meaning so that when this form is then employed in a context where it is not normal, it brings in some of the flavour of this original setting. (Blom and Gumperz, 1972: 425)

In this passage, Gumperz speaks of the semantic value of CS relative to what he calls 'metaphorical CS', but there is no doubt that it can be observed in the case of situational CS as well. In fact, other scholars (e.g. Auer, 1984) have questioned the distinction situational versus metaphorical CS for this very reason. A typical example of the directionality (semantic value) of metaphorical CS is Extract 2.1 below. The extract was recorded by Gal (1979) during her study of language shift in Oberwaert. The languages involved are Hungarian (italic characters) and German (bold). The general sociolinguistic situation is that of language shift from Hungarian to German. In other words, the situation can be described as that of diglossia whereby Hungarian is the (L)ow language and German the H(igh) variety. In the example, a grandfather asks his two grandchildren to stop what they are doing and come to him. Initially, he uses Hungarian, but as the children resist his request, he ups the stakes by switching to German, thus drawing on the social power of the language to give further strength to his request.

Extract 2.1 (Gal, 1978, cited in Gafaranga, 2007b)

Grandfather: *Szo! Ide dzsüni! (pause) jeszt jerámunyi*
               (Well, come here! Out all this away)
               mind e kettüötök, no hát akkor! (pause)
               (both of you, well now)
               kum her! *(pause) Nëm koapsz vacsorát*
               (**Come here!**) you don't get supper

On the other hand, the following example, taken from Myers-Scotton's (1998) study of language choice in East Africa, can be used by way of illustrating the semantic effect in situational CS. The sociolinguistic context of the example is Kenyan bilingualism, a situation which, following Mkilifi (1978), can be described as 'double-overlapping diglossia' (Fasold, 1984), with English and Swahili as the H languages and they-codes, and the various local languages as the L languages and we-codes. In the specific examples, the languages involved are Swahili (H) and Lwidhako (L).

Extract 2.2 (Myers-Scotton, 1988)

At the entrance of an IBM head office in Nairobi. The visitor, who is from the Luyia area of western Kenya, approaches and addresses the security guard.

Security Guard (Swahili):   Unataka kumuwona nani?
                              (Who do you want to see?)

Visitor (Swahili):   Napenda kumwona Solomon
                              Inyama.
                              (I want to see Solomon
                              Inyama.)

Security Guard (Swahili):   Unamujua kweli? Tunaye
                              Solomon A — Nadhani ndio
                              yule.
                              (Do you really know him?

	We have a Solomon Amuhaya — I think that's the one you mean.)
Visitor (Swahili):	Yule anayetoka Tiriki — yaani Luyia. (The one who comes from Tiriki — that is, a Luyia person.)
Security Guard (Luyia):	Solomon menyu wakhumanya vulahi? (Does Solomon know you?)
Visitor (Luyia):	yivi mulole umuvolere ndi Shem Lusimba — venyanga khukhulola. (You see him and tell him that Shem Lusimba wants to see you.)
Security Guard (Luyia):	Yikhala yalia ulindi. (Sit here and wait)
(At this point another visitor comes in)	
Visitor (Swahili):	Bwana K — yuko hapa? (Is Mr Kamidi here?)
Security Guard (Swahili):	Ndio yuko — anafanya kazi saa hii (talk goes on in Swahili). (Yes he is — he is doing something right now)

At the beginning of the interaction, participants do not know each other and normatively choose Swahili as the *medium of their interaction* (Gafaranga and Torras, 2001). That is, for participants themselves, Swahili is the they-code, the appropriate variety to use when a non-solidary relationship obtains between participants. In the course of the interaction, they recognise each other as coming from the same region of Kenya where Lwidhako is used. To signal this mutual recognition and claim co-membership of the same tribal group, participants switch from speaking Swahili to using Luyia, the we-code. Thus, social information is communicated metaphorically, i.e. without explicitly formulating it.

Note, however, that Gumperz is quick to emphasise that, in bilingual conversation, not every instance of CS can be interpreted in terms of we- / they-code: 'In many (. . .) cases it is *the choice of code itself in a particular conversational context* which forces interpretation' (1982: 83; original emphasis). This point is made even more explicit by Auer (1995: 124), according to whom contextualisation cues may lead to inferences either by 'contrast or by inherent meaning potential'. In the first and simplest case, 'the mere fact of (usually abruptly) changing one (or more than one) formal characteristics of the interaction may be enough to prompt an inference about why such a thing happened.' Clearly, in this case, the meaning of CS is situated in the realm of talk organisation. In the second case, contextualisation cues indicate contrast, but they also at the same time restrict the number of possible plausible inferences as to what this might be. This is so because cues may have (received) an inherent meaning potential. In this case, the meaning of CS is worked out by drawing on existing social conventions. Extracts 1 and 2 above illustrate this second possibility. As for examples of the first possibility, the reader is referred to Alfonzetti (1998: 186–206), who devotes a whole section of her paper on situations in which 'the direction of switching does not matter.'

Gumperz's account of CS may be, and indeed has been, criticised in its detail, especially at the level of the positive news it proposes. For example, based on a study of language practices among British-born Caribbeans in London, Sebba and Wootton (1998) came to the conclusion that the contrast we- / they-code, whereby these are fixedly assigned to specific languages, is too simplistic. In the study, different languages, notably London Jamaican and London English, are found 'to have some of the characteristics of "we-"codes' (1998: 264). Likewise, in a study of Italian dialect code-switching in Sicily, Alfonzetti (1998) came to the conclusion that, in their data, it was 'not possible (. . .) to assign to each code a semantic value, like for instance that of "we-code" and "they-code"' (1998: 207). However, the negative news that Gumperz has delivered – namely, that, when it comes to bilingual language use, 'things are not as they appear' – has not been questioned. Rather, scholars have largely embraced this position and gone on to suggest alternative explanations, to tell alternative positive news. In the sections below I survey two such developments. As I have indicated above, Gumperz delivered the negative news statement in the context of a larger theory of interaction. Both developments I will survey below focus specifically on CS. Also, in order to appreciate these developments fully, it is important to keep in mind that, according to Gumperz, a contextualisation cue may have an 'inherent meaning' just as it may mean by mere contrast. The two developments below focus on one or the other of these two aspects of contextualisation cues.

2.3   Code-switching and the negotiation of interpersonal relationships in interaction

Drawing on Gumperz's view that CS, as a contextualisation cue, has an inherent meaning, and particularly on the view that, in a bilingual community, language varieties are conventionally associated with specific social values and identities (see we- / they-code), Myers-Scotton (Scotton, 1983, 1988; Myers-Scotton, 1993b, etc.) developed a model of CS which she alternatively termed 'the markedness model of codeswitching' and the 'rational choice model of codeswitching'. As indicated above, unlike Gumperz, whose aim was to develop a general theory of interaction, Myers-Scotton's motivation was to draw on available theories and develop an account of language alternation in bilingual conversation. She states her aim as follows:

> What is the engine that drives speakers to select one linguistic variety over another? Why speak English rather than Spanish while discussing a deadline with a fellow worker if you're both Chicanas in Los Angeles? (Myers-Scotton and Bolonyai, 2001: 1)

And, more specifically, 'what *motivates* speakers to switch languages within the same conversation?' (Myers-Scotton and Bolonyai, 2001: 6; emphasis added). Note the phrasing of Myers-Scotton's programmatic question. According to Myers-Scotton, the question is not whether CS is motivated or not, rather that it is assumed, taken for granted, that CS is motivated. The implication is, of course, that, being motivated, CS cannot be seen as a random phenomenon. In other words, in the case of Myers-Scotton, there is no need for an explicit negative news statement on CS and it is in this sense that her work can be seen as a development from / relative to Gumperz. In turn, this allows Myers-Scotton to focus on the positive news aspect more than Gumperz could have.

In theory, Myers-Scotton's programmatic question is neutral as to its potential answer. All sorts of potential motivations for CS are, in principle, open to investigation. In reality, however, Myers-Scotton has a preference and she does not hide it. For her, language choice is always socially motivated: 'any code choice points to a particular interpersonal balance (obtaining between participants)' (1988 / 2000: 138). And, indeed, one of her most important publications on the topic of codeswitching is significantly entitled *Social Motivations for Codeswitching* (1993b). In other words, Myers-Scotton's (negative and positive) news

statement can be formulated as: *CS is not random because it contributes to social meanings in interaction.* This is stated more or less explicitly by Myers-Scotton as follows:

> While conveying referential information is often the overt purpose of the conversation, all talk is also a negotiation of rights and obligations between speaker and addressee. Referential content – what the conversation is about – obviously contributes to the social relationships of participants, but with content kept constant, different outcomes may result. This is because the particular linguistic variety used in an exchange carries social meaning. (1988 / 2000: 137–8)

A good illustration of how all this works can be found in Extract 2.3 below.

Extract 2.3 (Myers-Scotton, 1988 / 2000)

Passenger *(Lwidakho)*:	(*speaking in a loud voice and joking voice*) Mwana weru, vugula khasimoni khonyene (Dear brother, take only fifty cents)
	(*Laughter from conductor and other passengers*)
Passenger *(Lwidako)*:	Shuli mwana wera mbaa (Aren't you my brother?)
Conductor *(Swahili)*:	Apana . . . mimi si ndugu wako. Kama ungekuwa ndugu wangu ningekujua kwa jina. Lakini sasa sikujui wala sikufahamu (No, I am not your brother. If you were my brother, I would know you by name. But, now I don't know

	you or understand you.)
Passenger (Swahili):	Nisaidie tu bwana. Maisha ya Nairobi imenishinda kwa sababu bei ya kila kitu imeongezwa. Mimi ninaketi Kariobang'i, pahali ninapolipa pesa nyingi sana kwa nauli ya basi (Just help me, mister. The life of Nairobi has defeated me because the price of everything has gone up. I live at Kariobang'i, a place to which I pay much money for the bus fare.)
Conductor (Swahili):	Nimecukua peni nane pekee yake (I have taken 80 cents alone)
Passenger (English / Swahili):	Thank you very much. Nimeshukuru sana kwa huruma ya huyu ndugu wango (I'm very grateful for the pity you showed me, my brother)

The exchange takes place on board a bus in Nairobi (Kenya). In the extract, referential content, more precisely the on-going interactional activity, is the negotiation of a favour to pay a reduced bus fare, something which could, in other contexts, be construed as corruption. For this activity to succeed, some 'felicity conditions' (Searle, 1969) must obtain. Notably, a specific social relationship must obtain between the driver and the passenger (preparatory condition). In the text, this is encoded by the referential words 'brother' versus 'mister'. Success or failure of this negotiation will in turn confirm that relationship. If the undertaking succeeds, a brother-to-brother relationship will be confirmed as the one obtaining between the passenger and the conductor. On the other hand, if it fails, a more distant relationship (mister-to-mister) will have been confirmed. In the event, even after the bus conductor has denied being a brother to the passenger (turn 3), when the favour is granted, he is treated as a brother (turn 6). That is to say, social relationships are negotiated through the transactional level of talk and, at the same time, they contribute to it. In the process, language choice is drawn on as an additional resource. The passenger and the bus conductor come from the same region of Kenya (Luyia) where Lwidhako is used. In the Nairobi context, in public places such as a bus full of passengers, Swahili would normally be the expected choice. In using Lwidhako, the passenger is highlighting the shared tribal identity and, by so doing, maximising his chances of success. On the other hand, by using Swahili, the conductor rejects the claimed shared identity (at least for the benefit of the over-hearing audience). This in turn frees him up actually to grant the favour while appearing, in the eyes of other bus users, to be acting in the open and therefore not to be involved in corruption. Briefly, in this particular case, the choice to use either Swahili or Lwidhako is demonstrably motivated. The social meanings the language varieties are associated with are exploited for the purposes of the interaction at hand.

Keeping this basic premise that language choices are indexical of specific rights and obligations between participants, Myers-Scotton enlists a number of theoretical frameworks and develops her Markedness Model of Codeswitching, later reformulated as the Rational Choice Model (Myers-Scotton and Bolonyai, 2001). The first major theoretical framework that Myers-Scotton has drawn on is the Social Exchange Theory, especially the Rational Choice Model (Green, 2002). In its simplest form, the Rational Choice Model holds that, in social action, individuals are always faced with a choice to make between different alternative courses of action. In deciding which of the alternatives available to adopt, individuals anticipate and balance the costs and rewards of each (Green, 2002; Scott, 2000). These costs and benefits may be material but they may also be symbolic. The influence of this theory of social action on Myers-Scotton's account of language choice in social interaction is explicitly expressed in the following: 'I argue that a major motivation for using one variety rather than another as a medium of interaction is the extent to which this choice minimises costs and maximises rewards for the speaker' (1993b: 100). Elsewhere, she confirms this view, saying that 'To switch codes is a *calculation* that the anticipated interpersonal rewards codeswitching will yield are greater than those that initiating or maintaining a monolingual discourse pattern can confer' (1999: 1259–60; emphasis added).

These ideas of language choice as a balance between anticipated costs and rewards are beautifully illustrated in Extract 2.3 above. In this situation, the interactants are faced with the choice between adopting the neutral passenger–conductor relationship and using Swahili, and the more solidary tribesman–tribesman relationship and using Lwidhako. Interestingly, the calculation of the optimal course of action leads to different decisions. The passenger figures out that his request for a reduced fare stands a better chance of success if the solidary relationship is adopted. On the other hand, the conductor's own calculation leads him to conclude that adopting the solidary relationship in the presence of other passengers would be too costly. Goffman's (1981) distinction between 'addressed recipients' and 'unaddressed recipients' is a useful one here.

A key assumption in Rational Choice Theories and in Myers-Scotton's model of code-switching is that, before social action is accomplished, different alternatives are available to actors. In the case of CS, the assumption is that speakers have access to the two or more languages involved (Meeuwis and Blommaert, 1998). This assumption pervades Myers-Scotton's writing. For example, in her programmatic questions, one can read: 'What is the engine that drives speakers *to select one linguistic variety over another?*' (emphasis added). Likewise, in her statement of the main motivation for CS, we can read: 'I argue that *a major motivation for using one variety rather than another* as a medium of interaction is the extent to which this choice minimises costs and maximises rewards for the speaker' (1993b: 100; emphasis added). Such statements, in the context of rehabilitating CS, are very significant. The reader will recall that, previously, CS had been seen, among other things, as reflecting speakers' lack of competence in one or both of the languages involved (see Chapter 1). What is being stated here is the exact opposite. Rather than being seen as resulting from lack of competence, access to – that is, competence in – the two languages involved is assumed. Previous commentators 'have got it wrong'.

A second theoretical framework that Myers-Scotton draws on is the Markedness Theory. Markedness is a theory of oppositions and is used in various disciplines, including different branches of linguistics (e.g. voiced versus voiceless phonological sounds, count versus non-count nouns, definite versus indefinite article, etc.). Myers-Scotton extends the same idea to language choice among bilingual speakers, and argues for a distinction between marked and unmarked language choices.[1]

The markedness model (. . .) claims that, for any interaction type and the participants involved, and among available linguistic varieties, there is an 'unmarked choice.' (. . .) Discourses including CS are no different; that is, they also show an 'unmarked choice'. (1997: 231)

Central to Myers-Scotton's argument is the notion of *interaction type* or *conventionalised exchange.*

A conventionalised exchange is any interaction for which speech community members have a sense of 'script'. They have this sense because such exchanges are frequent in the community to the extent that at least their medium is routinized. That is, the variety used or even specific phonological or syntactic patterns or lexical items employed are predictable. In many speech communities, service exchanges, peer-to-peer informal talk, doctor–patient visits, or job interviews are examples of such conventionalized exchanges. (1998 / 2000: 138)

In a conventionalised exchange, there normally is a fit between language choice and the rights and obligations set obtaining between participants. Fishman uses the term *congruence* for this fit between language choice and social situations (Fishman et al., 1971). When there is congruence between language choice and the rights and obligations set, language choice is said to be unmarked, and when there is no congruence between the two, language choice is said to be marked. Consider Extract 2.2 above again. In the extract, two visitors have approached the guard. Each time, the guard has elected to use Swahili when talking to them as if by default, as if following a pre-existing script. The choice of Swahili is unmarked in this context. A second good example of 'script-like' behaviour in language choice among bilingual speakers is Extract 2.4 below.

Extract 2.4

1. A: mpe mperutse no kubona ntuza avuga ho avuga
        kuri *télévision* (.) simenya (.) *ministre* wa
        finance
2. B: {to child} *papa a dit papa a dit va t'asseoir
        là-bas*
3. Ch: *non*
4. B: {to child} *si si c'est ce que papa a dit
        parce que tu as fait des bêtises*
5. A: umh R ni nde ra R
6. C: eh warayibonye
7. B: {to child} *là-bas là-bas*

8. A: jye narayibonye (.) sinzi ukuntu nafunguye
        hano mbona agezweho
9. Ch. *là là*
10. B: {to child} *tu as fait des bêtises*
11. C: jye buri gihe saa mbiri n' igice (.) ndeba
        kuri ART

----

1. A: I recently saw that man talking on *television*
        (.) I don't know (.) *finance minister*
2. B: {to child} *papa said papa said go and sit
        there*
3. Ch: *no*
4. B: {to child} *yes yes that's what papa said
        because you've been naughty*
5. A: umh R who's he R
6. C: eh did you watch it
7. B: {to child} *over there over there*
8. A: I watched it (.) I switched on just like this
        and there he was
9. Ch: *over there*
10. B: {to child} *you've been naughty*
11. C: every 8:30 (.) I want ART

The wider sociolinguistic context of this extract is that of language
shift from Kinyarwanda–French language alternation to French in the
Rwandan community in Belgium, as described in Gafaranga (2010,
2011). In this community, it is routine practice for adult members to
choose French when speaking to children and to choose Kinyarwanda–
French language alternation when speaking to other adult members.
This particular conversation takes place in a family setting with children
around. A is the host and father of the Child (Ch). B and C are friends
who are visiting. As the transcript shows, on this occasion, the routine is
re-enacted afresh. B uses French every time he has to talk to Ch and he
uses Kinyarwanda when he talks to the adult participants. And the navi-
gation between the languages as B's interlocutors change is quite seam-
less. Again, in this case, we will say that language choice is unmarked.

Extract 2.3, on the other hand, shows a situation where language
choice is marked. As we have seen, the conversation takes place in a
public space, namely on board a bus in Nairobi. In this situation, the
choice of Swahili is unmarked. On the contrary, the choice of Lwidhako
by Passenger is marked, indeed remarked upon by everybody present.

As the transcript shows, right after Passenger's first turn, other passengers laughed. The question here is: what are they laughing at? What is incongruous in this situation? Two possibilities are, in principle, available: it may be what Passenger has said, just as it may be how he has said it. Referential content has to be excluded for two reasons. To start with, Lwidhako is not accessible to everybody such that they would have understood what Passenger has said. In fact, one reason Passenger has chosen this language is to exclude the other passengers. Secondly, referential content (talk about the relationship between Passenger and Conductor) is actually maintained throughout the extract, but laughter stops after Passenger's first turn. So we ask: what has changed for the situation to normalise and stop being incongruous? Only language choice has changed. The medium has changed from Lwidhako to Swahili, the predictably unmarked choice. Therefore we have to conclude that the incongruity has to be the choice of Lwidhako. Thus, in this context, the choice of Lwidhako is demonstrably marked. A further example of a marked language choice can be seen in Extract 2.5 below.

Extract 2.5

A civil war, reportedly Rwanda-instigated, has just erupted in Zaire (present-day Democratic Republic of Congo) and home to hundreds of thousands of Rwandan refugees. Participants are talking about the consequences this is going to have on these refugees.

```
1. A:      ubu rero ab (.) buretse (.) abazayuruwa
           bagiye gutangira ngo (.) fukuza munyar-
           wanda (.) [( )
2. B:      [avec raison (.)[puisque turi imbwa
3. A:      [( ) ((laughter)) ariko
4. C:      avec raison (.) none se none wanzanira
           ibibazo iwanjye
```

```
1. A:      now Zairians Zair (.) wait a minute (.)
           Zairians are going to start saying kick
           out Rwandan (.) [( )
2. B:      [rightly so (.) [as we do not deserve
           any respect
3. A:      [( ) ((laughter)) but
4. C:      rightly so (.) if you bring problems to
           my door
5. A, B, C: ((laughter))
```

The conversation involves three adult Rwandan friends in Belgium in an informal context. Therefore, Kinyarwanda–French language alternation is the unmarked choice. Can the use of Swahili in turn 1 be seen as marked and in what sense? Participants' behaviour will give us important clues. In turns 3 and 5, participants engage in the non-verbal activity of laughing. As in the previous case, we ask: what are they laughing at? A turn-by-turn analysis reveals the following: in turn 2, B reacts to the referential content of A's talk and agrees with him. However, overlapping this agreement, A laughs. In turn 4, C too orients to referential content and agrees with both B and A. In 5, all three participants laugh together. As referential content has been fully worked up (total agreement has been reached), one has to ask what this chorus response through laughter responds to. Working back to turn 3, we can analyse A's laughter as a 'technique for inviting laughter' (Jefferson, 1979). As Jefferson has demonstrated, in order to invite laughter from interlocutors, a current speaker may place a laughter token right after they have completed an utterance. The next question then is: what is A inviting interlocutors to laugh at? The fact that fellow Rwandans are being forced back to Rwanda at gunpoint is certainly no laughing matter. Rather, what is being proposed as a source of amusement is the choice of Swahili on this occasion and whatever that choice is meant to achieve (see Chapter 4 for a complete analysis of this extract). In other words, in this case, the choice of Swahili is marked and is meant to be recognised as such.

Having argued that there are two basic types of language choice – namely, marked and unmarked language choices – and having claimed that, to make one or the other of the two types of choice, speakers follow the principle of optimal return, Myers-Scotton must now answer the questions of what is to be balanced and where it is to be found. The answer to the first question is that balancing takes place, not between languages per se, but between the social values associated with them. She speaks of the *social indexicality* of language varieties in bilingual communities. As we have seen, according to Myers-Scotton, 'all linguistic code choices are indexical of a set of rights and obligations holding between participants in the conversational exchange.' In addition, speakers would be aware of the indexical value of the language varieties as part of their '*communicative competence*' (Hymes, 1972; Gumperz, 1972).

> Speakers have a tacit knowledge of this indexicality as part of their communicative competence. (. . .) The result is that all speakers will have mental representations of a matching between code choices and rights and obligation sets. That is they know that for a particular conventionalised exchange, a certain choice will be the unmarked realisation of an

expected rights and obligation set between participants. (Myers-Scotton, 1988 / 2000: 152)

Myers-Scotton refers to this type of communicative competence as the *markedness metric* and, alternatively, as the *markedness evaluator*. Extracts 2.2 and 2.3 above point to the reality of this social indexicality of language choices and to speakers' awareness of it. Even Extract 2.1, from a completely different sociolinguistic context, can be used as further evidence of this indexicality.

As we have seen, Myers-Scotton's model of CS is a development from Gumperz's earlier work. Both scholars share the opinion that there is a conventional relationship between language and society, based on the view that 'language reflects society' (Cameron, 1990; Gafaranga, 2005). As a result, the model brings along some of the problems associated with those earlier views. For example, as we have seen, one issue in Gumperz's approach is known as the directionality of language alternation. Inevitably, the same problem arises in the Markedness Model of CS due to its notion of the social indexicality of language choices. While it is true that some choices are indexical of the social values society associates with the language varieties used, others are not. Compare the following two examples from the same sociolinguistic context.

Extract 2.6

1. A: hee (.) *donc* nkora muri *lexicologie* (.) *plus
       précisément kuri compétence lexicale* muri
       école secondaire
2. B: umh
3. A: ( ) *je me suis limité aux* **premières années**
       (.) **imyaka ya mbere**
4. B: umh
5. A: kuko nkeka *hypothèse* yanjye ni uko iyo abana
       bavuye muri *primaire* nta gifaransa baba bazi

----

1. A: yes (.) *so* my work is in *lexicology* (.) *pre-
       cisely* on *lexical competence* at *secondary
       school level*
2. B: umh
3. A: ( ) I *have limited myself to* **the first years**
       (.) **first years**
4. B: umh
5. A: for my *hypothesis* is that when children

graduate from *primary school* they do not know French

Extract 2.7

```
1. A:  mpa dusangire
2. B:  kuko twe twakoreshaga iminsi ibiri hafi n'igice
       (.) deux jours et demi
3. C:  eh nzi nzi abantu bavaga iwacu kakajya kwiga
       (.) iZaza (.) n'amaguru
4. A:  umh
5. C:  bakoreshagaa icy (.) [icyumweru cyose
6. A:                       [icyumweru

----------------------------

1. A:  let's share
2. B:  as for us we used to walk for about two days
       and a half (.) two days and a half
3. C:  eh I know people from my village who used to
       go to school (.) in Zaza (.) on foot
4. A:  umh
5. B:  they would walk for a whole week
6. A:  a week
```

Both extracts come from conversations involving Rwandans in Belgium. In both cases, the highlighted elements involve reiteration for emphasis. However, in 2.6, the direction of switch is from French to Kinyarwanda, while in 2.7 it is from Kinyarwanda to French. It would appear that, in this case, what matters is not so much what values the languages are associated with at the level of the community, but rather, as Gumperz had observed, the mere fact of juxtaposing the languages. Also consider the following from Milroy and Wei (1995):

Extract 2.8 (Milroy and Wei, 1995)
Conversation between two women in their early forties in the Chinese community in Newcastle.

```
A:  . . . . Koei hai ysaang
    [He's a doctor]
B:  Is he?
A:  Yichin (.) hai Hong Kong
    [before] [In Hong Kong]
```

As Milroy and Wei rightly argue, the choice of English here, after the use of Chinese, functions to highlight the repair initiator (also see

Chapter 5) by contrast rather than by the inherent social meaning with which English is associated. A summative way of referring to this kind of problem is that, among bilingual speakers, language choice does not necessarily reflect society (Gafaranga, 2005).

A second issue in Myers-Scotton's positive news has to do with the nature of the evidence used in support of claims and how it is generated. This is important if we keep in mind that, as Heap (1990) observes, positive news is primarily addressed to 'professional' scholars. This issue is elegantly captured by Wei (1998). Wei describes the Markedness Model of Codeswitching as an 'analyst-oriented' perspective whereby researchers 'bring along' their own assumptions in their analysis of the data, rather than approaching CS with an attitude of indifference and examining the meaning of CS as it is 'brought about' in the details of the interaction. Take, for example, the identification of an instance of language choice as either marked or unmarked. Should an instance be identified as marked based on the analyst's ethnographic knowledge or should it be identified as such based on participants' own orientation as revealed in the details of talk? Based on what we know about the sociolinguistic situation of Kenya, the use of Lwidhako in Extract 2.3 can be concluded to be marked. Likewise, based on what we know about the sociolinguistic situation of the Rwandan community in Belgium, the choice of Swahili in Extract 2.5 could be concluded to be marked. Swahili is not normally used in this community. However, there is a slight problem here. As our analysis has shown, participants have not automatically viewed the choice of Swahili as marked. Indeed, B and C initially reacted to referential meaning, paying no attention to language choice. It is only after A has used the specific technique of inviting laughter, as described above, that the markedness of the choice of Swahili became apparent and was reacted to as such. To be sure, even the choice of Lwidhako in Extract 3 can be re-analysed as marked, not because of what we know about the wider sociolinguistic context, but because of the way participants have reacted to it in the local context of the talk. Take another example. The extract below comes from a conversation involving British-born Caribbeans in London. In this context, as we have seen, none of London English and London Jamaican can be considered as the definite we-code. Therefore, here, it is impossible to tell a priori which of the two languages is the unmarked choice and which is the marked choice. Yet a detailed analysis of language choice, as conducted by Sebba and Wootton (1998), reveals a significant contrast. London English is used as the base medium of the interaction and is associated with the current speaker and his interlocutors. Against the background of this basic medium, London Jamaican stands out and is *consistently* used to denote (negatively) the actions of 'this black man'. In other words, London Jamaican is marked, not because of what we know about the languages in the community, but against the background of London English.

Extract 2.9 (Sebba and Wootton, 1998)

```
F:  Yeah man, I was on the till on Saturday (1.2) and
    this this black man come in (1.0) and (0.6) you
    know our shop, right, (0.6) they u:m (0.2) give
    (.) refund on (0.3) Lucozade bottles (0.4)
G   M:
F   a black man come in an' 'im b(h)u::y a bottle (.)
    of Lucozade while 'e was in the shop [an'
G                                        [free p-e's e got free pee off is it?
F   Yeah
G   Small ones or big ones?
F   big ones and 'e drank the bottle in fron2 of us
    an then ask(d) for the money back (see man) me
    want me money now
G   [heheh
F   [he goes (pnk) (I'm on) the till guy (.) hhh (I
    jus) (0.6) I jus' look round at 'im (0.6) I said
    well you can't 'ave it (1.9) I said I 'ave to
    open the till (w) wait till the next customer
    comes (1.0) 'now! open it and gi' me de money'
    (1.0) I said I can't (0.8) the man just thump
    'is fist down an' (screw up dis for me) (.) (s no
    man) the manager just comes (.) 'would you leave
    the shop before I call the security' hh the man
    jus' take the bottle an' fling it at me an (I) jus
    catch it at the (ground)
```

Thus, there is a tension among scholars as to whether analytic categories such as marked / unmarked should be analysts' constructs or whether they should be participants' own categories.

2.4   Code-switching and talk organisation

The conversation analytic approach to CS, developed by Auer (1984, 1988, 1995), promises to overcome the above two problems found in the Markedness Model. On the issue of the directionality of CS, Auer states that 'code-switching is not necessarily related to a metaphoric function (in Gumperz' sense). *Often, it 'just' takes part in the organisation of discourse* (1988 / 2000: 185; emphasis added). And, on the issue of whether analytic categories should be participants' own, he says that it is 'the users (of CS) who decide on (its) status' (1995: 117). More concretely, he writes:

> the procedures we aim to describe are supposed to be those used by participants in actual interaction, i.e. (. . .) they are supposed to be interactionally relevant and 'real', not just as a scientific construct designed to 'fit the data'. So there is a need for an analytic interest in members' methods (or procedures), as opposed to an interest in external procedures derived from a scientific theory. In short, our purpose is to analyse members' procedures to arrive at local interpretations of language alternation. (1984: 3)

What does a conversation analytic approach to CS look like, then? To answer this question, we need to be clear about Conversation Analysis (CA) itself. According to practitioners, CA is the study of 'the order / organization / orderliness of social action, particularly those social actions that are located in everyday interaction, in discursive practices, in the sayings / tellings / doings of members of society' (Psathas, 1995: 2). Furthermore, according to conversation analysts, in conversation, those actions are organised sequentially, i.e. one after the other. As Goffman puts it metaphorically, CA investigates the 'syntactical relations among the acts of different persons mutually present to one another' (1967: 2). The fact that conversation is organised sequentially is an important resource for analysts. Analysts can look at how participants have reacted, in the talk itself, to co-participants' contributions and 'witness' participants' own meanings, thus avoiding the problem of 'bringing along' their own assumptions (Wei, 1998). Another way of putting this is that CA adopts an 'emic' perspective (Pike, 1967). Consider Extract 2.10 below, from a general practice consultation.

Extract 2.10 (Gafaranga and Britten, 2005)

1. D: So what can I do for you then?
2. P: Oh
3. D: What's the problem?
4. (0.2)
5. P: I've got rashes

The on-going action is a request by the doctor to the patient to disclose the reason for the surgery visit. This opening sequence has a specific organisation. It consists of two *first concern elicitors* (Gafaranga and Britten, 2003): namely, 'What can I do for you?' and 'What's the problem?'. These two first concern elicitors are not juxtaposed; they are separated by P's 'Oh'. That the two actions by D are separated by P's 'Oh' is very significant. Because of this intervening 'Oh', D's action in turn 3 is understood to have been undertaken for a particular reason, namely the failure of his first action to elicit an appropriate reason for the visit. In turn, structurally, this is so because '(. . .) what can I do for you?' is a *first pair part* in an *adjacency pair* (Schegloff and Sacks, 1973). In an adjacency pair, after a first pair part, current speaker must stop speaking and next speaker must, at this point, provide a relevant *second pair part*. In this case, 'Oh' is not a relevant second pair part. Therefore, because 'what can I do for you?' has not received a relevant second pair part, D produces a *'second attempt'* (Auer, 1984) at eliciting P's consulting concern. Conversation analysts speak of a *third place repair*. To appreciate this, we can think of an alternative ordering whereby D would have produced both concern elicitors one after the other without P's 'Oh'. In this case, D's action would be analysable as having been motivated, not by the lack of a response on the part of P, but by his own realisation of the inappropriateness of his first concern elicitor. In this case, conversation analysts would speak of a *transition space repair*.[2] That is to say, the meaning, and indeed the nature, of a language item, as social action, depend on its position in the sequence of actions.

Auer acknowledges the CA influence on his work on more than one occasion. His very definition of bilingualism is as a set of activities, rather than a property of the mind.

> bilingualism is no longer regarded as something inside the speaker's head, but as a displayed feature in participants' everyday behaviour. You cannot be bilingual in your head, you have to use two or more languages 'on stage', in interaction, where you show others that you are able to do so. So I propose to examine bilingualism primarily as a set of complex linguistic activities (. . .). (1988 / 2000: 169; my emphasis)

The meaning of CS is explicitly claimed to be dependent on its sequential environment and Auer's analysis to consist of sequential analysis.

> any theory of conversational code-alternation is bound to fail if it does not take into account that the meaning of code-alternation depends in essential ways on its 'sequential environment'. This is given, in the first place, by the conversational turn immediately preceding it, to which code-alternation may respond in various ways. While the preceding verbal activities provide the contextual frame for current utterance, the following activities by a next participant reflect his or her interpretation of the preceding utterance. Therefore, following utterances are impor-

tant cues for the analyst and for the first speaker as to if and how a first utterance was understood. (1995: 116)

The sequential nature of CS (or code alternation, as Auer calls it) can be witnessed if we look at *language negotiation sequences* (Auer, 1995), especially at *medium requests* (Gafaranga, 2010). Consider Extract 2.11 below.

Extract 2.11

```
1. B:  Ni nde wakwigishije?
2. C:  Moi toute seule
3. B:  Toute seule?
4. C:  Les copines qui m'ont montrée
```

```
1. B:  Who taught you to do it?
2. C:  (I learned) all by myself
3. B:  (you learned) all by yourself?
4. C:  Some friends showed me (how to do it)
(Conversation continues in French)
```

To say that the meaning of CS depends on its sequential environment means that, in this particular case, we note that the choice of French in turn 2 contrasts with that of Kinyarwanda in the immediately preceding turn and that, from this point onward, talk proceeds in French. More specifically, B's adoption of French in turn 3 indicates that he has interpreted C's choice of the same language in turn 2 as a request to adopt French as the medium. In other words, language choice in turn 1 serves as a background against which language choice in turn 2 is seen as noticeable, while language choice in turn 3 and onward reveals how first speaker has interpreted co-participant's alternating action.

Of course, CS need not be observed across turns for it to be sequential. It can also take place within the same speaker's turn. Consider Extract 2.12.

Extract 2.12

```
1. C:  Yuu! Mwali nka bangahe? (.) Vous étiez combien
       à peu près?
2. E:  Toutes les filles ou tout le groupe?
3. C:  Tout le- tout le groupe a dansé?
4. E:  Pas tout le- tout le groupe
```

```
1. C:  Yuu ! How many were you roughly? (.) How many
       were you roughly?
2. E:  All the girls or the whole group?
3. C:  Did the- the whole group dance?
4. E:  Not the- the whole group
```

In this example, C says something in Kinyarwanda and then repeats it in French. Here, the choice of Kinyarwanda in a first *turn constructional unit* (TCU) (Sacks et al., 1974) serves as the background against which the choice of French in the second TCU becomes visible. As for the interpretation of this case of CS, we look at subsequent talk. In this particular case, we note that, from turn 2 onwards, French was adopted as the medium. Thus the interpretation of this instance, as Gafaranga (2011) notes, is as a *transition space medium repair*: that is, as an offer to adopt French as the medium. Along the same lines, language choice in Extracts 2.6 and 2.7 can be seen as sequential, although, in this case, given the participants' subsequent behaviour, the interpretation of this action of language alternation must be seen as different.

So far we have looked at CA as a method we can use in investigating bilingual conversation. But CA is more than a methodology. As its definition indicates, CA has a specific object. CA is the study of talk organisation. How does CS relate to talk organisation then? According to Auer,

> In the organization of bilingual conversation, participants face two types of tasks. First, there are problems specifically addressed to language choice. A given conversational episode may be called bilingual as soon as participants orient to the question of which language to speak. Second, participants have to solve a number of problems independently of whether they use one or more languages; these are problems related to the organization of conversation in general, e.g. turn-taking, topical cohesion, 'key' (. . .), the constitution of specific linguistic activities. The alternating use of two languages may be a means of coping with these problems. (1988 / 2000: 170)

Thus Auer's positive news may be phrased as follows: CS is not random because participants use it as a 'means of coping with problems in conversation', notably those 'related to the organization of conversation in general' (Auer, 1988 / 2000: 170).

By way of an illustration of the two types of problem participants involved in a bilingual conversation may face, consider Extract 2.13 below.

Extract 2.13 (Torras, 1999, cited in Gafaranga, 2005)

```
1. STU:  I'm sorry it's not your fault right
```

```
2. SEC:  no [uh no that's you— you— you—
3. STU:  [I'm erm I offended you
4. SEC:  mmm (.) LE LE DROIT LE (to RES) el dret
5. RES:  the right
6. SEC:  the right (.) you have the right to protest
         eh OK
```

```
4. SEC:  mmm (.) the the right the (to RES) the right
```

In this interaction, participants have adopted English as the medium. In turn 4, SEC faces a 'problem specifically addressed to' the choice of this language. More precisely, she experiences difficulties in continuing the conversation in this language. She runs across the problem of the *mot juste* in English for what she wants to say. To solve this problem, she needs help from co-participants. In turn, this leads to the *self-initiated other-repair problem* (Gafaranga, 2012; also see Chapter 5). That is to say, she faces the problem of telling co-participants exactly what it is that she is having problems with so they can help solve it. To overcome this difficulty she switches from English to French. That is to say, CS from English to French occurs in the context of a problem related to the medium partici-pants have chosen to use. However, as the on-going is a multi-party con-versation, a second, and entirely different, problem arises. An important issue in multi-party conversation is that of turn-taking: notably, that of assigning the right to speak next. According to Sacks et al. (1974), current speaker selects next speaker and, if not, next speaker self-selects. In the first possibility, a number of different resources that current speaker may use in selecting next speaker are available (e.g. naming, gaze, gesture, etc.). In the case at hand, CS from English to Catalan is used.

Of course, the two types of problem do not always co-occur in every instance. In some instances, CS is addressed to one or the other of the two problems. For example, in Extract 2.11, the relevant issue is solely that of language choice. The evidence for this is the fact that turn 2 is a relevant second pair part even though, at the level of language choice, the choice of French is a non-sequitur relative to the imme-diately preceding use of Kinyarwanda. On the other hand, consider Extract 2.14.

Extract 2.14 (Milroy and Wei, 1995)[3]

(Dinner-table talk between mother A and daughter B; Chinese, English)

```
1. A:  oy-m-oy faan a? A Ying a?
       [Want or not rice?]
```

```
2. B:  (No response)
3. A:  Chaaufaan a. Oy-m-oy?
       [Fried rice. Want or not?]
4. B:  (2.0) I'll have some shrimps
5. A:  Mut-ye? (.) Chaaufaan a
       [What?] [Fried rice]
6. B:  Hai a
       [Okay]
```

Milroy and Wei (1995) rightly analyse the use of English as addressed to a problem strictly 'related to the organization of conversation' (Auer, 1988 / 2000: 170), notably as CS for marking dispreference. In this case, there is no issue of the medium of interaction, or at least there is no evidence of such an issue. On the contrary, evidence in the talk points to Chinese being the agreed medium (see turns 5 and 6) and to English being only an additional dispreference marker, others being the silence in turn 2 and the (2.0) pause in turn 4. As Auer (1995: 124) notes, 'contextualisation cues often bundle together.' (Also see the notion of 'double marking' in Gardner-Chloros et al., 2000.)

Alongside the two different types of task / problem participants in a bilingual conversation deal with, Auer identifies two different types of CS – namely, *participant-related* and *discourse-related code alternation* – and associates the latter types with the former types more or less explicitly. Notably, discourse-related CS is said to be 'for certain conversational tasks which are relevant in monolingual contexts as well' (1988 / 2000: 174). In other words, discourse-related code alternation is addressed to problems that participants face 'independently of whether they use one or more languages', i.e. 'problems related to the organization of conversation in general' (1988 / 2000: 170). Conversely, it is implied, participant-related code alternation is addressed to issues related to language choice, i.e. to medium-related issues. In an attempt to clarify this distinction between participant-related and discourse-related switching further, Auer writes:

> If we compare participant and discourse-related language alternation we note that the main difference is the object of the signalling process. Whereas in the case of participant-related alternation, co-participants display or ascribe certain predicates to each other (competence, preference), they signal a change of conversational context in the case of discourse-related switching. (1988 / 2000: 176)

Consider Extract 2.14 again. As we have just seen, in the instance, there is no evidence that CS to Chinese is due to competence / preference in one or the other of the languages involved. Indeed, available evidence is that both participants are competent (for all practical purposes) in the two languages. Conversely, in Extracts 2.11, 2.12 and 2.13, there is evidence that CS is due to language preference / competence.

It is worth commenting further on this distinction between participant-related and discourse-related language alternation. As we have seen earlier, a problem in language alternation studies is the language competence assumption, the assumption that CS presupposes competence in the languages involved (Meeuwis and Blommaert, 1998). In formulating the distinction between participant-related and discourse-related language alternation, Auer acknowledges the possibility that CS need not be premised on the participants' full competence in the languages involved. CS may occur precisely because of knowledge gaps in one of the languages involved. Also, quite interestingly, according to Auer, only discourse-related code alternation, the one which presumes competence in the two languages, fits Gumperz's definition of a contextualisation cue (Auer, 1988 / 2000: 176). As a result, this raises the question of whether participant-related CS, the type of language alternation addressed to issues which arise at the level of the medium, can be seen as random. Auer acknowledges the scarcity of studies which address this type of language alternation, but suggests that it too, or at least some of it, can be seen as orderly because it is sequential (1995: 127). This is the type of language alternation that participants adopt by way of negotiating the medium of interaction (language negotiation sequence). Extract 2.11 above is a good example. However, it is important to recognise an inherent problem in this explanation. One type of language alternation (discourse-related) is said not to be random because of what it does for participants (contribution to talk organisation) while the other (participant-related) is said not to be random because of its surface organisation (sequentiality).

As we have seen, the starting point for Auer's positive news is the observation that there are two types of problem in bilingual conversation: namely, problems to do with language choice and problems to do with talk organisation in general. An alternative point of departure may be thought of. As Gafaranga (1999) argues, language choice itself is a significant aspect of talk organisation'. Furthermore, arguably, medium-related issues arise both in monolingual and in bilingual conversation. In other words and to paraphrase Auer, problems at the level of the medium may be thought of as problems of 'talk organization in general'. Given this respecification, the distinction between participant-related and discourse-related language alternation becomes descriptively irrelevant. Rather, Gafaranga (2007b: 148) proposes the

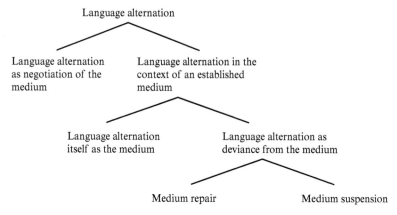

Figure 2.2   Categories of language alternation

categorisation of language alternation phenomena shown in Figure 2.2. In this view, the positive news is: CS is not random because it contributes to talk organisation (whether at the level of the medium or at the level of other interactional activities).

2.5   Where to from here?

As indicated in the Introduction, studies of language alternation have been undertaken against the background of negative attitudes towards bilingualism and towards CS in particular. Therefore, the research tradition so far can be described as a rehabilitation effort. A specific perspective in this rehabilitation effort is the sociofunctional perspective. Along with other perspectives such as the grammatical account, its main achievement is to have delivered what, in Heap's (1990) terms, can be termed 'negative news'. That is, the literature has amply demonstrated that those previously held negative attitudes were unfounded. Drawing on a variety of research paradigms, scholars in this perspective have gone beyond merely delivering negative news and proposed positive news. It has been argued that CS is not random because it functions as a contextualisation cue, that it contributes to the negotiation of interpersonal relationships in interaction and that it contributes to talk organisation. The correctness of each of these formulations of the positive news may be debated; indeed, no one account meets everybody's assent. In the future, debates may continue at the level of the general theories of language alternation and improvements may be proposed, but there is no guarantee that one universally agreed-upon model of CS will ever be produced. And this should not be surprising because CS, like any other aspect of language use, is always multi-dimensional. So where to from here? As the discipline has largely achieved its initial goal of rehabilitating CS, how can it continue to be relevant and interesting? In this book a possible direction for future work on bilingual language use is proposed. In line with Auer (1984), the proposed direction starts from the view that bilingualism consists of diverse interactional practices and works towards an 'accumulation of empirical findings about those (. . .) practices' (Heritage and Clayman, 2010: 14). That is to say, rather than developing yet another general theory of bilingual language use, the aim of this book is to encourage researchers to begin to 'grapple with some small bit(s) of the world (i.e. bilingual language use) in order to get an analytic handle on how (they) work' (Sidnell, 2010: 1). Chapter 3 establishes the methodology for investigating bilingualism as interactional practices before later chapters can instantiate it.

Notes

1. To be sure, Myers-Scotton detailed these broad categories to make finer ones, but here I will limit myself to these two.
2. See Chapter 5 for a more developed discussion of repair in conversation.
3. Turns numbered for convenience.

3 An inductive perspective on bilingualism as interactional practices

3.1 Introduction

The aim of this chapter is to establish a methodology which can be adopted in investigating bilingualism as interactional practices. In Section 1.4, it was indicated that such a methodology should be inductive in nature. This is partly due to the diversity of potential practices and, as a result, to the impossibility of prescribing a relevant theory for each. An inductive attitude allows for data to be explored empirically and for explanations to be developed as the data dictate. Also, for the purpose of mainstreaming the study of bilingual language use, the methodology should be such that it can be applied to bilingual data and to monolingual data as well. Given these requirements, at this point, I can only state in broad lines the general methodological positions which I think can be fruitfully applied, independently of the actual practice under investigation. The chapter starts with these broad lines of methodology before illustrating them with a monolingual example.

From its conception, CA has been understood as the study of interactional practices, of conversational practices, to be sure. Unsurprisingly, therefore, CA provides us with the basics of a methodology we can adopt and adapt in describing interactional practices, conversational or not, monolingual and bilingual alike. The methodology, discussed at length in Pomerantz and Fehr (1997), Ten Have (1999), Sidnell (2014) and others, is known as the study of collections and comprises the following main steps:

1. notice a phenomenon
2. collect a corpus of what seem to be instances of the phenomenon
3. conduct a case-by-case analysis to establish whether each item is indeed an instance of the phenomenon
4. generate hypotheses as to the organisation of the practice as you go
5. identify prototypical instances, variations and deviations

6. propose a structural account for variation and a functional explanation for deviation.

In the following paragraphs, I comment on some of the most salient features of this methodological proposal.

Anybody with any degree of experience in supervising developing researchers will agree with me that identifying researchable topics is one of the most challenging tasks for them. Even when they have access to a corpus of data, let alone when they have to collect that corpus themselves, they are often at a loss as to what to look for. Simply put, they do not notice anything about those data. Fortunately, time-tested advice is currently available, namely that topics for current research are often inspired by previous research. In this respect, Cameron is very right when she writes:

> most 'good ideas' for research do not just spring from the researcher's imagination, they are suggested by previous research (. . .). Knowledge of any subject is cumulative: people look at what is already known and notice gaps (. . .), or think of objections (. . .) or supplementary questions. (Cameron, 2001: 182)

Alternatively, especially for more experienced researchers, an interesting idea may 'spring from' the data through repeated observation.

Both situations are illustrated in the case studies included in this book. For example, as will become clear later, the proposed description of language choice in speech representation (Chapter 4) started from previous work by researchers who had noticed and reported that, among bilingual speakers, language alternation often co-occurs with direct speech reporting. Moving beyond this noticing, I raise the 'supplementary question' of the exact nature of the relationship between speech representation and language choice in bilingual conversation. Conversely, the description of translinguistic apposition, as proposed in Chapter 6, can be seen as starting from my own observation of the data. Indeed, as far as I am aware, nobody had previously investigated translinguistic apposition, and certainly not in the Rwandan context. However, even in the latter case, the role of the researcher's familiarity with the literature cannot be underestimated. The specific phenomenon was noticed as potentially interesting against the background of the knowledge already existing about 'most highly regulated texts' (Sebba, 2002), namely that language alternation is, in principle, impossible in such texts. Briefly, in investigating bilingual interactional practices, topics may develop either from the researcher's familiarity with current literature or from his / her own observation of the data.

In the list above, 'steps' 2 to 6 are presented as if they were discrete and ordered. It is as if one did 2, before 3, before 4, before 6 and so on. Nothing could be more untrue. In reality, these steps are interrelated and interdependent. For example, an instance is identified as an instance of something (2) only because a working definition (hypothesis) (4) of that something exists. In turn, given a working definition, an item is identified as an instance of something by confirming that it fits the definition (3). An instance is identified as fitting the definition because it is either a typical case, a variation or a deviation (5). In turn, an instance is confirmed to be either a variation or a deviation depending on whether a structural account or a functional explanation can be found. Briefly, the list can be seen only as a convenient, but reductionist, way of talking about the various actions that the researcher must accomplish, not necessarily one after the other. It is in this sense that the term 'exploration' of the data seems to me to be a very apt description of what the researcher actually does. It is hoped that, working through the cases reported in this book, the reader will be able to recognise the different actions in each case.

Step number 6 is particularly interesting for it points to the need to account for the totality of the data. Data, interactional data in particular, are almost always variable. As a result, typically, the aim of analysis is to demonstrate that this variability is not random, that there is order – that is, regularity – in diversity. In turn, to demonstrate regularity, data are typically approached from either of two perspectives, namely a positivistic perspective and an interpretivistic perspective. The positivistic perspective, associated with quantitative methods, sees regularity in terms of frequencies. A typical example of a positivistic perspective in language studies can be found in variationist sociolinguistics, as practised by Labov and others. For example, in his study of *The Social Stratification of English in New York*, Labov (1966) observed phonological variability at the level of 'th' in words such as 'then' and 'those'. Sometimes it was realised as an explosive (dh) (as in 'den' and 'dose') and sometimes as a fricative (standard pronunciation). Statistical analysis of the data revealed patterning at two levels: the level of social class and that of speech style (A for casual style, B for careful style and C for reading style) as in Figure 3.1. The higher the social class was, the more often the standard pronunciation was found, and the more formal the style was, the more often the standard pronunciation was used by all classes.

However, it is important to note that 'the variants (were) not associated exclusively with one class or another. Middle-speakers use some [d] . . . and working-class and lower-class speakers (used) some [đ]. It

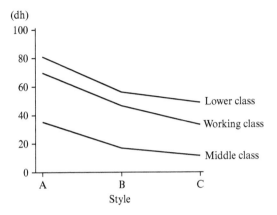

Figure 3.1   Stratification of (th) in New York City (Labov, 1966: 221–2)

(was) only the *relative frequencies* that (were) stratified' (Fasold, 1990: 224;
emphasis added). The limit of such an account of the choice between
[d] and [đ], as a social practice, is obvious. Some individual members of
a social class may score above or below their class average. How is this
behaviour going to be accounted for? One way of going beyond such
averages is to use the notion of social network (see, for example, Milroy,
1980; Gal, 1979; Wei, 1994, etc.) and explain individuals' behaviour in
terms of the social contacts they regularly engage in. However, even
this may not be enough, as individuals may deliberately move in and
out of their social network norms. As Garfinkel (1967) says, individuals
are not 'cultural dopes', whose behaviour merely reproduces the norms
of their respective communities. Along the same lines, Gumperz (1981:
325) says that 'Many sociolinguistic studies (...) aim at little more
than statements of regularities that describe the occurrence of utterances or verbal strategies in relation to types of speakers, audiences,
settings and situations.' It is at this level, where an account is sought
for each and every instance of the data, rather than for general trends
within the data, that the positivistic perspective must be abandoned in
favour of the interpretive perspective, a perspective which recognises,
among other things, individuality and agency. A typical example of this
concern for accounting for the totality of the data is Schegloff (1968). It
is reported that, having collected 500 instances of conversational openings, Schegloff refused to settle for any generalisation about the structure of conversational openings which did not apply in each and every
one of the 500 instances. In turn, each and every one of the 500 instances
was accounted for either as normative or as accountable deviance from
the norm. It is such an interpretive approach which I propose to adopt

in investigating interactional practices involving the use of two or more languages. The case study below illustrates this inductive methodology for investigating interactional practices, without the further complication of language choice.

3.2 A monolingual example: doctor-initiated 'howareyou' sequences in GP consultations

3.2.1 Introduction

The opening phase of the medical interview has retained the attention of many scholars, especially medical educationalists with an interest in communication skills (Pendleton et al., 1984, 2003; Neighbour, 1987; Silverman, Kurtz and Draper, 2005, etc.). According to these scholars, the two main interactional activities in this phase are (1) establishing initial rapport and (2) identifying the reasons for the consultation. The same phase has also been investigated by conversation analysts (Heath, 1981; Gafaranga and Britten, 2003, 2005; Ruusuvuori, 2000, 2005; and Robinson, 2006). These researchers have specifically focused on the second interactional activity, namely the elicitation of the reasons for the consultation, also known as *patients' presenting concerns*, and identified a number of devices, referred to as *first concern elicitors* (Gafaranga and Britten, 2003 and 2005), that doctors use in eliciting patients' presenting concerns. These include questions such as 'what can I do for you?', 'what's up?', 'how are you feeling?', 'how are you?' and so on (see Gafaranga and Britten, 2005: 79, and Silverman et al., 2005: 43, for a short list). Furthermore, researchers have shown that the choice among the various first concern elicitors is not random, but rather that it is rule-governed.

Of particular interest among these devices that doctors use to elicit patients' presenting concerns is 'how are you?' and its variants (hereafter the form *howareyou* will be used to refer to the type, keeping the standard orthography for specific instances). *Howareyou* is interesting because researchers do not agree on its nature. While some (e.g. Heath, 1981; Gafaranga and Britten, 2003, 2005) maintain that *howareyou* is a first concern elicitor, others (e.g. Robinson, 2006) do not. Indeed, according to Robinson, unlike proper first concern elicitors, *howareyou* 'does not, in and of itself, index patients' institutionally relevant concerns' (2006: 39). The fact that, in everyday conversation and indeed in other types of institutional talk, *howareyou* is 'geared towards sociability rather than instrumental tasks' (Heritage and Clayman, 2010: 63) adds to the confusion. Therefore, an empirical question is: what exactly is the nature of *howareyou* in doctor–patient interaction? According to Robinson, *howareyou* would get to be 'produced and understood as a solicitation of patients' presenting concerns (...) through specific interactional practices other than turn design' (2006: 39). Exactly what are those practices? Thus, the aim of this case study is to contribute to this debate by investigating these two specific questions: (1) in doctor–patient interaction, is *howareyou* a first concern elicitor or is it not? (2) If it is not, what interactional practices do participants deploy in sequences where *howareyou* looks as if it was a first concern elicitor?

The following extracts of talk can be looked at by way of an initial appreciation of the issues involved in the use of *howareyou* in doctor–patient interaction:

Extract 3.1 (B0514C)[1]

1. P: **How are you?**
2. D: Fine thanks. And you?
3. P: Very well
4. D: Have a chair. Have you got the form?
5. P: Yes

Extract 3.2 (B0104C)

1. D: And **how are you today** {first name}?
2. P: Well you can see that I've still got my pain so—
3. D: Yes. Yeah ((uses computer)) Pain is still
     there is it?
4. P: Yeah

As the transcripts show, an initial distinction which can be made is between patient-initiated (as in Extract 3.1) and doctor-initiated (as in Extract 3.2) *howareyou* sequences. As the on-going topic is whether *howareyou* is or is not a first concern elicitor, our focus will be on doctor-initiated sequences. Secondly, in Extract 3.1, *howareyou* is used, as in ordinary everyday conversation, as a general enquiry about the participants' current state of being (Schegloff, 1986: 126), as evidenced by the neutral responses 'fine' and 'very well' (Sacks, 1975), and by the fact that it is reciprocated (see below). In Extract 3.2, on the other hand, *howareyou* seems to function as a first concern elicitor. P displays the reason he is visiting the surgery as if in response to the doctor's 'How are you today?'. In other words, to use a distinction by Brown and Yule (1983), *howareyou* serves an *interactional* function in the first extract and it seems to have a *transactional* meaning in the second.

However, not all doctor-initiated *howareyou* are responded to with a statement of the presenting concerns. Consider Extract 3.3 below:

Extract 3.3 (L0214C)

```
1. D:  Right. How are you Mrs R?
2. P:  All right thank you
3. D:  How do you feel?
4. P:  Yes (0.2) yes. Very lonely
5. D:  Coping? Yeah? I'm not sure you are
```

In this extract, P meets D's 'How are you Mrs R?' with a neutral response ('All right thank you') as in ordinary everyday conversation. That is, here, 'How are you Mrs R?' has been taken to have an interactional meaning. It is because doctors' *howareyou* seems to serve two different functions in doctor–patient interaction that the questions above arise and must be addressed.

As a number of authors (Drew and Heritage, 1992; Drew and Sorjen, 1997; Heritage, 1997; Heritage and Greatbatch, 1991; Kasper, 2009, etc.) have indicated, everyday conversation forms the 'benchmark' against which institutional talk is understood. Accordingly, we will start, in Section 3.2.2, with a discussion of the main properties of the *howareyou* sequence in everyday conversation. Section 3.2.3 will situate the present analysis in its research context, looking at previous work on the use of *howareyou* in doctor–patient interaction. In turn, this review will allow me to contextualise the research questions as stated above. These questions will then be addressed in Section 3.2.4. In that section, in line with Robinson (2006), I will show that *howareyou* is not a first concern elicitor as such, and why. I will also show that, through the specific interactional practices of *pre-emption* (Schegloff, 1986) and *forestalling*, doctors and patients accomplish talk in which *howareyou* looks like a first concern elicitor. The data come from a corpus of 62 general practice consultations collected in the Midlands and the South-east of England (see Stevenson et al., 2000, for a description of the study design).[2] In addition to this data set, I will draw on extracts of talk from the literature in illustrating general aspects of the organisation of *howareyou* sequences.

3.2.2   Howareyou *in everyday conversation*

Researchers have highlighted the importance of a comparative perspective in the study of institutional talk. In turn, this is based on the view that ordinary everyday conversation 'constitutes a kind of benchmark against which other more formal or "institutional" types of interaction are recognized and experienced. (. . .) institutional forms of interaction (. . .) show systematic variations and restrictions on activities and their design relative to ordinary conversation' (Drew and Heritage, 1992: 19). Therefore, in the following, I discuss some of the most relevant features of the *howareyou* sequence in ordinary everyday conversation so that I can later on use them as points of reference in examining the organisation of doctor-initiated *howareyou* sequences.

The *howareyou* sequence has been investigated mostly in the opening phase of telephone conversations, but, as Liddicoat (2007: 253) puts it, 'In face-to-face conversations, . . . the opening is quite similar to that found in telephone openings (. . .).' More specifically, according to Kendon and Ferber (1973; as cited in Liddicoat, 2007), in face-to-face conversation, the *howareyou* sequence occurs and, as in telephone conversation, it commonly follows the exchange of greetings. Extract 3.4 below shows the opening of a telephone conversation:

Extract 3.4 (Liddicoat, 2007)

```
          ((ring))
Chris:  Hello:?
Dan:    Hi Chris?
Chris:  Hi Dan, how're you
Dan:    Okay, How're you doin.
Chris:  Can't complain
```

Extract 3.5, on the other hand, is an opening sequence of a face-to-face interaction – namely, a GP consultation:

Extract 3.5 (B0205C)

```
1. P:  Hello there Dr L
2. D:  Hello there. Come in
3. C:  [Hello
4. D:  [Hello. How are you doing?
5. P:  All right. ((grunts)) ((Door closes))
```

The two openings are significantly similar. The only major difference between the two is that, while *howareyou* is reciprocated in Extract 3.4, it is not in Extract 3.5. However, even in telephone conversations, *howareyou* is not always reciprocated (see below). Therefore, although the following comments are mostly based on work on telephone conversations (following Schegloff, 1968, 1986, 2000), they are assumed to be valid for face-to-face conversations as well. In addition, where possible, I will also use data from my corpus of general practice face-to-face consultations – notably, patient-initiated *howareyou* sequences – to highlight the similarities.

i. Summons / answer sequence
ii. Identification (and / or recognition) sequence
iii. Greeting exchange sequence
iv. Howare you sequences
v. Anchor position

Figure 3.2   Phases of the opening in telephone conversation

A typical telephone opening, according to Schegloff (1968, 1986, 2007), has the five phases shown in Figure 3.2. Extract 3.4 above shows all these phases. The ringing and Chris's first turn constitute the summons / answer sequence; Dan's first turn and Chris's 'Hi Dan' constitute the greeting sequence and the identification–recognition sequence, and the rest of the extract consists of two sequences each made up of *how-areyou* and its response. After this exchange of *howareyous*, the anchor position – that is, the slot for a first topic – opens up. Briefly, the *how-areyou* sequence is the fourth component in the opening sequence. Its function is, as Schegloff (1986: 118) puts it, to provide 'a formal early opportunity for the other party to make some current state of being a matter of joint priority concern'. This can be seen in Extract 3.6 below.

Extract 3.6 (Pridham, 2001)

((ring))

```
1. Bhavini:  hiya
2. Philip:   hiya (2) how are you?
3. Bhavini:  I'm alright ((laughs))
4. Philip:   You're alright
5. Bhavini:  just woke up
6. Philip:   yeah
7. Bhavini:  vegged for a bit
8. Philip:   right
```

(talk goes on with Bhavini telling her story)

In this telephone conversation, Philip is the caller. Therefore, he is entitled to the first topic, the reason for the call. However, by uttering 'how are you?' in turn 2, he offers Bhavini the opportunity to have her pressing concerns, if any, talked about before the reason for the call. As we can see, this opportunity is indeed taken up by Bhavini, who describes how she is feeling. It is because, in everyday conversation, as in the example above, *howareyou* is used for the purposes of socialising, is 'geared towards sociability rather than instrumental tasks' (Heritage and Clayman, 2010: 63), that it can be said to have an essentially interactional function.

The first structural property of the *howareyou* sequence is that it is an *adjacency pair sequence* (Schegloff and Sacks, 1973) in which the *howareyou* form is the *first pair part* and the answer is the *second pair part*. As Schegloff (1986: 129) says, *howareyou* 'make(s) an answer a relevant next turn'. Three types of answers are possible after *howareyou*: neutral answer, negative answer and positive answer. The choice among these three options has, as we see below, important organisational consequences. If a neutral answer is chosen, the sequence usually consists of two turns (first pair part and second pair part) and it may optionally take a *minimal post-expansion* (Schegloff, 2007) in the form of a *closing third* (Sacks, 1975). Both situations are found in the following extract.

Extract 3.7 (Sidnell, 2010)

```
           <<ring>>
01 Anne:   =Hello::
02 Jane:   Oh=hi_=it's Janet_[Cathy's mom]
03 Anne:               [hi:  jane]
04         How eryou(h).h hh
05 Janet:  I'm goo:d, how are y|ou
06 Anne:   [I'm fi:ne h[we're actually:uhm:
07 Janet:  [° good °
08         (0.2)
```

The extract comprises two *howareyou* sequences (see below for a description of the relationship between the two components). In line 4, Anne utters *howareyou* and, in line 5, Janet responds to it with 'I'm goo:d' and goes on immediately to open the second sequence. In line 6, Anne responds to this second *howareyou* with 'I'm fine.' And, in 7, Janet acknowledges this response using 'good'. For a second example, consider the following patient-initiated sequence. As the transcript shows, this sequence is, in every respect, similar to the second sequence above.

Extract 3.8 (L0103C)

```
1. P:  (0.2) How are you?
2. D:  I'm okay {first name}
3. P:  Good (0.3) Long day again
```

Because the *howareyou* sequence is an adjacency pair sequence, it can be expanded by means of insertions and / or by means of post-expansions. For the first case, it is not very difficult to imagine a situation (e.g. in the case of lack of hearing) where a *post-first insertion* (Schegloff, 2007) would occur. However, more interesting for the concerns of this section is the possibility of post-expansions. As we have seen above, in the case of a neutral second pair part, a minimal post-expansion is possible, as in Extracts 3.7 and 3.8 above. In the case of a non-neutral (either positive or negative) second pair part, on the other hand, a *non-minimal post-expansion* (Schegloff, 2007) is almost the preferred course of action. In this respect, Schegloff writes:

> 'Positive' and 'negative' responses engender sequence expansion; they take up the opportunity to engage in talk on that topic. Ordinarily, they prompt in their recipient (the asker of the 'howareyou' question) a request for an account of the state they have announced (e.g., 'what happened?'). (Schegloff, 1986: 129)

An example of this is given in Extract 3.9 below, where Sam's positive answer 're:ally great' triggers Kim's query 'why?', this in turn leading to Sam's answer.

Extract 3.9 (Liddicoat, 2007: 241)

```
     ((ring))
     Kim:   Hullo.
     Sam:   Hi !
→ Kim:   Hi How're you:.
→ Sam:   Re:ally grea:t.
→ Kam:   Why?
     Sam:   Well I just had some really good news..
```

In this respect, an interesting situation arises in Extract 3.6 above. In the extract, Bhavini responds to Philip's 'how are you?' using 'I'm alright', a seemingly neutral response. However, she signals the insincerity of her response non-verbally by laughing. Philip understands the meaning of this signal and calls for an account of the now-negative response.

The *howareyou* sequence can be expanded but it can also be extended. By *extension*, I mean the fact that the basic sequence is completed and then recycled in some form or other. There are two basic procedures for extending the *howareyou* sequence, namely by means of *reciprocal or exchange sequences* and by means of *same action-type sequence series*. Schegloff (2007: 195) defines reciprocal or exchange sequences as 'episodes in which a sequence which has just been initiated by A to B (that is, in which A is the first pair part speaker and B is the second pair part speaker) is then (after it has run its course) reciprocated – initiated by B to A'. That is to say, at the completion of the first adjacency pair sequence, a new one may be launched, the producer of the first *howareyou* becoming the receiver of the second. Extract 3.7 above is a good telephone example and here is a face-to-face example:

Extract 3.10 (B0514C)

```
1. P:  How are you?
2. D:  Fine thanks. And you?
3. P:  Very well
4. D:  Have a chair (. . .)
```

As for the same action-type sequence series, it occurs when

> the same sequence type is done again – more precisely another instance of the same sequence type is done, with the same parties as first pair part and second pair part speaker(s), but with a change in topic or target of the sequence. (Schegloff, 2007: 207)

In the extract below, the first sequence ends with Ava's minimal expansion ('that's good') and, right after, she launches a new sequence which differs from the first only at the level of the subject of the enquiry ('Bob' rather than 'you').

Extract 3.11 (Schegloff, 2007)

```
1. Ava:  →  [°(Any way).] [hh] How'v you bee:n.
2. Bee:     hh oh : : survi : ving I guess, hh [h!
3. Ava:                  [That's good, how's
4.          (Bob),
5. Bee:     He's fine,
6. Ava:     Tha : : t's goo : d,
```

Researchers such as Saadah (2009) have argued that this type of extension of the *howareyou* sequence is common in Arabic-speaking communities but, clearly, it is not limited to them.

As part of the opening, the *howareyou* sequence can be pre-empted. Schegloff (1986: 133) defines pre-emption as the fact of shortening the opening sequence by initiating the 'first topic or some initial action sequence before the opening has worked itself out in full'. In Extract 3.12 below, Kate pre-empts the *howareyou* sequence by reporting the difficulty she has experienced in her previous attempts to reach Ann rather than responding to Ann's 'how are you?'.

Extract 3.12 (Liddicoat, 2007)

```
        ((ring))
Ann:    He : llo:,
```

```
Kate:  Hi Ann.
Ann:   Hello . How're you?
Kate:  I've been trying to ring you a : ll da:y.
Ann:   Oh I w' z working today.
Kate:  o : hh. I[thou-
Ann:        [ I hadden extra shift.
Kate:  yeah, Iknew that you were usually at home today.
Ann:   So Whaddid you want?
```

In the example above, pre-emption works to block the second pair part after *howareyou*. But pre-emption may also occur later and block either expansions or extensions of the basic sequence. Consider Extract 3.13 below:

Extract 3.13 (Liddicoat, 2007)

```
          ((ring))
Sally:  Hello:,
Sam:    Hello!
Sally:   Hi Sam,
Sam:    How are yuh.
Sally:  Fine, how're you
Sam:    hhhh oh not so good.I had this real problem
        today at work.
Sally:  Wha' happ'n' d.
```

As we have seen, negative answers like Sam's 'not so good' '(o)rdinarily (. . .) prompt in their recipient (the asker of the "howareyou" question) a request for an account of the state they have announced (e.g. "what happened?")' (Schegloff, 1986: 129). In this case, Sam embarks on the account for her negative response even before Sally formulates the request for it and, by so doing, makes the request lose its relevance.

To summarise, in everyday conversation, and in mundane telephone conversation in particular, the *howareyou* sequence, by enquiring about the current state of the participants, provides 'each party with an opportunity to introduce some pressing matter in advance of the reason for the call' (Heritage and Clayman, 2010: 62). The basic sequence consists of a first pair part (a form of *howareyou*) and a second pair part (response). In turn, three possibilities are available for the second pair part, namely a neutral response, a positive response and a negative response. These three types of second pair part are not equivalent structurally. While both the negative response and the positive response lead to non-minimal post-expansions in the form accounts of the states of affairs announced, the neutral response may, but need not, lead to a minimal expansion in the form of a closing third. The basic sequence may be extended either through reciprocation or through same action-type series. And, finally, the sequence can be pre-empted by initiating another action sequence before it has run its full course. In the sections below, I will examine doctor-initiated *howareyou* sequences, using these properties of the sequence in mundane talk as 'the bench mark' (Drew and Heritage, 1992: 19).

3.2.3   The howareyou *sequence in doctor–patient interaction*

Schegloff (2007: 202) notes that *howareyou* sequences 'are not relevant in certain types of institution-specific conversations' and that, where they are observed, they may be organised differently from one institution to the next. For example, as Whalen and Zimmerman (1987) and Zimmerman (1992) have shown, in emergency calls, the *howareyou* sequence is one of the opening steps which are routinely absent. Likewise, *howareyou* sequences are reported to be absent in the opening phase of news interviews (Clayman and Heritage, 2002: 66). On the other hand, describing their data consisting of 'interactions between customers and employee' at 'Eastside Reprographics', Vinkhuyzen and Szymanski (2005: 106) write that these interactions 'are not unlike phone call openings'. This can be read as implying that the *howareyou* sequence can be found in these service encounters. Indeed, one of the examples they use in their discussion of service requests reads as follows:

Extract 3.14 (Vinkhuyzen and Szymanski, 2005)

```
1. C:  Hello, [how are you?
2. E:          [Hi
3. E:  How [can I help
4. C:      [I've gotta make a copy of = uh this document.
5. E:  okay would you like to do that yourself in the
       do-it-yourself?
```

Finally, at a general level, Heritage and Clayman state the following of *howareyou* sequences in institutional talk:

> *how are yous* are generally absent (. . .) from impersonal occupational encounters of many kinds. When they do appear in such encounters, their presence can impart an element of sociability and warmth to what would otherwise be a purely instrumental transaction. Indeed, they may be exploited by telemarketers and other sales personnel (. . .) in an effort to establish a sense of personal relationship (. . .). (Heritage and Clayman, 2010: 63)

In the case of doctor–patient interaction, as the few examples we have looked at so far indicate, the *howareyou* sequence is a routine feature of talk. As we have seen, some *howareyous* are patient-initiated while others are doctor-initiated. Patient-initiated *howareyou* sequences can easily be understood as conforming to the above description, i.e. to be targeted toward sociability. And, as the examples we have examined show, they are organised in the same way as in everyday conversation. Can the same be said of doctor-initiated *howareyou* sequences? In other words, do doctor-initiated *howareyous* serve only an interactional role, as in the case of everyday conversation? Do they also serve a transactional role? Do the sequences in which doctor-initiated *howareyou* occurs show the same / different organisation as in / from everyday conversation?

Extract 3.5 above shows that doctors' *howareyou* can indeed serve an interactional function. As the transcript demonstrates, the patient meets the doctor's 'How are you doing?' with a neutral response, 'All right.' Also consider Extract 3.15 below (Extract 3.3 reproduced for convenience). Here, the doctor's *howareyou* is met with a neutral answer, this closing the *howareyou* sequence and opening the anchor position.

Extract 3.15 (L0214C)

```
1. D:  Right. How are you Mrs R?
2. P:  All right thank you
3. D:  How do you feel?
4. P:  Yes (0.2) yes. Very lonely
5. D:  Coping? Yeah? I'm not sure you are
```

Finally, consider Extract 3.16 below. In the example, the doctor uses *howareyou* and the patient replies using the neutral answer 'okay'. However, through laughter, both participants mark the situation as delicate (Haakana, 2001; Namba, 2011). Particularly, the patient's 'okay' is flagged as actually negative and this leads the doctor to initiate an expansion by means of the query 'okay?'. In other words, this example is similar in every respect to Extract 3.6, except for the participants involved.

Extract 3.16 (L0101C)

```
1. D:  Hello {first name}
2. P:  Hello
3. D:  How are — er how ((laughs))
4. P:  ((laughs)) I'm okay
5. D:  Okay?
6. P:  (melting). Saw {first name}. In fact [we went
       up to {a town}
```

```
 7. D:  [Oh yes
 8. P:  and her they've got a cottage at {S-village}
 9. D:  Ah nice
(9 turns omitted)
10. D:  right
```

Briefly, the first observation to be made is that doctor-initiated *howareyou* may be similar functionally and structurally to its counterpart in everyday interaction.

Secondly, as Extract 3.2 above (reproduced below as extract 3.17 for convenience) shows, a doctor's *howareyous* may lead to talk which looks as if it has been taken to serve a transactional function.

Extract 3.17 (B0104C)

```
1. D:  And how are you today {first name}?
2. P:  Well you can see that I've still got my pain so—
3. D:  Yes. Yeah ((uses computer)) Pain is still
       there is it?
4. P:  Yeah
```

A similar situation obtains in Extract 3.18 below.

Extract 3.18 (B0412C)

```
1. D:  Good. Right. How are you?
2. P:  Oh indigestion I've come about cos it gets
       worse at night. It's terrible
3. P:  Oh dear
```

Briefly, it is because of this apparent ambivalence of doctor-initiated *howareyou* that the issues regarding its actual nature, whether it is or is not a first concern elicitor, arise.

Doctor-initiated *howareyou* also raises organisational issues. In Extracts 3.17 and 3.18 above, patients display their presenting concerns immediately after doctors' *howareyous*. However, this need not be the case. The presenting concern may be delayed, as in Extract 3.19.

Extract 3.19 (L0610C)

```
1. D:  Here we go. How are you?
2. P:  Er I'm all right thanks. Er {first name} came
       up on (0.2) last night. Last night
3. D:  Right
4. P:  And she's gonna come up next Wednesday
5. D:  [Right
```

```
6. P:   [No not last night. Wednesday night. Sorry.
        And she's coming up next Wednesday after I've
        been here. Right. The reason I er come to see
        you on the third of May I'm going away for a
        week. I'm- I'm going to erm Greece and er I
        got to thinking about my ears. And erm I-I- I
        panicked a bit to be honest (. . .)
```

The issue therefore is: how are the sequences involving doctor's *how-areyou* organised? This is important because the organisation of those sequences might provide clues as to the nature of doctor-initiated *howareyou*. The section below investigates these two issues, that of the nature of doctor-initiated *howareyou* and that of the organisation of the sequences in which it appears. Before this, however, in the paragraphs below, I briefly look into the literature to see whether and how these issues have been addressed.

Interest in the opening sequence, and in doctor-initiated *howareyou* sequences in particular, can be found in two disciplinary camps, namely medical educationalists and (applied) conversation analysts. As Gafaranga and Britten (2005: 75–6) put it, 'From an educational perspective, interest in "opening gambits" stems from the realization that initial concern elicitors may mean more than they say.' The main concern for educationalists is to teach trainee doctors good practices, i.e. practices which allow 'patients to express their concerns in an unconstrained manner' (2005: 7). According to Silverman et al. (2005: 44), 'The format of the questions that we (doctors) use can subtly change the type of response that the patient provides.' In turn, this is hugely important because 'the manner in which patients present their problems (. . .) can have a variety of medical consequences' (Robinson, 2006: 22). Thus medical educationalists advocate the use of open questions, including those with the *howareyou* form (Silverman et al., 2005). That is to say, for medical educationalists, *howareyou* is only a first concern elicitor.

On the other hand, conversation analysts are interested in the *how-areyou* sequence in doctor–patient consultations as an interactional phenomenon, and their findings may, but need not, be used for teaching purposes (applied). In these conversation analytic studies of the *howar-eyou* sequence in doctor–patient interaction, three main claims can be observed. Heath (1981), in a very early investigation of GP consulta-tions in the UK, argued that *howareyou* is one of a pair of first concern elicitor types, the other type being '*whatcanIdoforyou*'.[3] According to Heath, *howareyou* is used to open a doctor-initiated consultation, while *whatcanIdoforyou* opens a patient-initiated consultation. Two decades later, Gafaranga and Britten (2003, 2005) revisited the issue of the opening sequence in the UK context and proposed a slightly different interpretation of the *howareyou* sequence and the *whatcanIdoforyou* sequence. Rather than focusing on who initiated the medical visit, they looked at how the presenting concern was interactionally constructed and found that a concern can be viewed either as on-going or as new. They spoke of a follow-up consultation in the first case and of a new consultation in the second. For new consultations *whatcanIdoforyou* was used and, for follow-up consultations, *howareyou* was used. Finally, using both American and British data, Robinson (2006) came up with yet another categorisation. He identified 'three different types of reasons for visiting physicians' (2006: 23): new concerns, follow-up concerns and chronic-routine concerns. To each of these there was a corresponding specific concern elicitor type. New concerns were elicited by means of the *whatcanIdoforyou* type, follow-up concerns required the *howareyou-feeling* type and routine concerns used the *what'snew* type. In addition to these, Robinson postulates a fourth category, the *howareyou* type. Describing this format, Robinson says that, unlike the others, *howareyou* 'does not, in and of itself, index patients' institutionally relevant concerns' (2006: 39).

From this rather sketchy review, two general points can be made. First of all, researchers, whether they are motivated by an educational agenda or by a strictly descriptive purpose, have focused only on those cases where doctors' *howareyou* seems to have a transactional value. As we have seen above, doctors may also use *howareyou* for interactional purposes. Because of this focus on one side, it has not been possible to settle the issue of the nature of doctor-initiated *howareyou* because the issue has not been properly raised in the first place. Secondly, conversation analysts have not focused on the sequential organisation of the sequences involving doctors' *howareyou* presumably because their main interest was to develop taxonomies of first concern elicitors. Even Robinson does not go beyond suggesting that doctors' *howareyou* can be 'produced and understood as a solicitation of patients' presenting concerns (through) interactional practices other than turn design' (2006: 39). Therefore, in the section below, an account of doctors' *howareyou* is proposed, one which, I hope, overcomes both limitations.

3.2.4 *The presenting concern as a pre-emptive and forestalling move*

As indicated in Sections 3.2.1 and 3.2.3, the first issue at hand is that of the nature of doctors' *howareyou* and whether it is or is not a first concern elicitor. A straight answer to this question is that doctors' *howareyou* is NOT a first concern elicitor. Four pieces of evidence can be offered in support of this position. First of all, as we have seen above, doctors' *howareyou* need not be responded to by stating the presenting concern. It may also be responded to with a statement of the patient's current general state of being (see Extracts 3.3, 3.5, 3.15, 3.16 and 3.19 above). Secondly, *howareyou* can co-occur with first concern elicitors, such co-occurrence not being viewed as involving repair. In Extract 3.15 above, one may argue that 'How do you feel?' is used because 'How are you Mrs R?' has failed to produce the expected results. That is, it can be argued that 'How do you feel?' is used because 'How are you Mrs R?' has not led to the display of the patient's presenting concern and, therefore, that it repairs it. However, the same cannot be said of the occurrence of 'What are we talking about?' in Extract 3.20 below (Extract 3.16 expanded). Rather, in the extract, the *howareyou* sequence seems to have run its full course, this leading to the *anchor position* (Schegloff, 1986).

> Extract 3.20 (L0101C)

```
 1. D:  Hello {first name}
 2. P:  Hello
 3. D:  How are — er how ((laughs))
 4. P:  ((laughs)) I'm okay
 5. D:  Okay?
 6. P:  (melting). Saw {first name}. In fact [we went
         up to {a town}
 7. D:                                      [Oh yes
 8. P:  and her they've got a cottage at {S-village}
 9. D:  Ah nice
(9 turns omitted)
10. D:  right
11. P:  What are we talking about today I don't know.
         I just feel slightly (0.3) a bit like a fraud
         I suppose. But I thought I'd have a word with
         you
12. D:  Mm
13. P:  Anything I eat
```

Given this, even Extract 3.15 can be re-analysed as a case where the *howareyou* sequence has run its full course before a first concern elicitor is produced. This lack of orientation to co-occurrence as repair suggests that *howareyou* and the first concern elicitors it co-occurs with do not do the same job.

Thirdly, as in everyday conversation, after a neutral response, current speaker may initiate a different action in the form of a pre-emptive move (see above), in this case displaying the reason for the visit, without this move being seen as cancelling the response. Here is an example:

Extract 3.21 (Gafaranga and Britten, 2005)

```
1. D:  Thanks for that. Sorry to keep you waiting so
       long.
2. P:  That's all right.
3. D:  Behind this afternoon. (0.2) How are you?
4. P:  Okay. Erm (could see) a couple of things
5. D:  Mm.
6. P:  And about my knee again but mainly erm I've been
       getting really bad headaches basically.
```

Also consider Extract 3.22 below.

Extract 3.22 (B0205C)

```
1. P:  Hello there Dr L
2. D:  Hello there. Come in
3. C:  [Hello
4. D:  [Hello. How are you doing?
5. P:  All right. ((grunts)) ((door closes)) Erm I'll
       tell you what I wanted to see you about
6. D:  Yeah
7. P:  You remember a long- well a- after I came out
       of hospital (. . .)
```

Fourthly, *howareyou* and other first concern elicitors do not occupy the same sequential position. As detailed in Schegloff (1986), the *howareyou* sequence follows the exchange of greetings and, crucially, precedes the anchor position. In Extract 3.23 below, after the *howareyou* sequence has been reciprocated, the caller announces the first topic, i.e. the reason for the call.

Extract 3.23 (Schegloff, 1986)

```
       ((ring))
Ida:   Hello,
```

```
Car:     Hi Ida
Ida:     yeah
Car:     Hi,=This is Carla
Ida:     Hi Carla.
Car:->   =How are you.
Ida:     Okay:.
Car:     Good.=
Ida:->   =How about you.
Car:     Fine Don Wants to Know. . .
```

Likewise, in Extract 3.24, at the completion of the *howareyou* sequence, the expectation was that P would announce a first topic, possibly the reason for the visit. As he has not, after a pause, D calls for the topic ('So') and P tables it in the next turn.

Extract 3.24 (L0104C)

```
1. D:    Right
2. P:    How are you?
3. D:    Okay thank you
4. P:    Good
         (0.4)
5. D:    So
6. P:    hh Right. Well I think I'm losing it basically
```

While *howareyou* leads to the anchor position, first concern elicitors occupy it. Extract 3.24 above is a good example. As we have just seen, D produces the first concern elicitor 'So' after noticing that the anchor position has not been occupied and thereby confirms that 'So' can validly occupy it. Likewise, in Extract 3.15 above, the first concern elicitor ('How do you feel?') occurred in the anchor position. Extract 3.25 below is a rather dramatic case. In the first three turns, the *howareyou* sequence is completed. Following this, two topics, invitation to sit down and enquiry about a consent form, are dealt with. And only then is the first concern elicitor ('What can I do for you?') produced.

Extract 3.25 (B05114C)

```
1. P:    How are you?
2. D:    Fine thanks. And you?
3. P:    Very well
4. D:    Have a chair. Have you got a form?
5. P:    Yes
6. D:    Right
```

```
7. P:   ((grunts))
8. D:   What can I do for you?
9. P:   Erm I've come to see you about my erm (...)
```

Incidentally, it is the fact that *howareyou* and first concern elicitors do not occupy the same sequential position which explains the possibility of co-occurrence without one being seen as repairing the other (see above).

Briefly, doctor-initiated *howareyou* is not a first concern elicitor and a variety of evidence supports this position: *howareyou* may co-occur with concern elicitors without this being seen as repair; *howareyou* need not be responded to by announcing the reason for the medical visit; the answer to *howareyou* may co-occur with the statement of the patient's presenting concern without there being repair; and, finally, *howareyou* does not occupy the same sequential position as first concern elicitors. If doctor-initiated *howareyou* is not a first concern elicitor, how come it occurs in sequences of talk which make it look like one? This is my second research question and it is to this that I now turn.

Given the fact that *howareyou* does not occupy the same sequential position as first concern elicitors and, therefore, the two can co-occur without there being repair, I want to suggest Figure 3.3 as the 'standard shape' (Drew and Heritage, 1992) for the opening of a doctor–patient interaction. Three observations can be made with respect to this standard shape. Firstly, this shape is consistent with models of the consultation, such as in Byrne and Long (1976) and Silverman et al. (2005), which distinguish the 'establishing initial rapport' phase from the 'identifying the reason(s) for the consultation' phase. Secondly, this shape is comparable to the one suggested by Schegloff (1968) for the opening of everyday telephone conversation (see above). The only significant difference is that, here, the first concern elicitor is seen as standard while the 'first topic elicitor' (Button and Casey, 1984) is optional in Schegloff's model. Finally, the shape applies in the case of doctor-initiated *howareyou* sequences, as well as in the case of patient-initiated sequences. Such an 'ideal' entry is actually realised in Extract 3.15 above. To some extent,

---

i.   (Summons)
ii. (Greeting / recognition)
iii. Howareyou sequences
iv. First concern elicitor
v.   Presenting concern

Figure 3.3   Standard shape of the opening in doctor–patient interaction

it is also realised in 3.25, if the intervening topics (invitation to sit and consent form) are bracketed off. It is this structure that I propose to use as a point of reference in answering the second research question.

As we have seen, Robinson (2006: 39) suggests that *howareyou* 'gets produced and understood as a solicitation of patients' presenting concerns (. . .) through interactional practices other than turn design', but he does not specify what those practices are. The display of presenting concerns after *howareyou* is as a result of two interactional processes: namely, *pre-emption* and what I may call, for the lack of a better term, *forestalling*. As we have seen above, Schegloff (1986) defines pre-emption as the process whereby the opening sequence is shortened by initiating another action before the sequence has run its full course. As for forestalling, the term is used here to refer to the fact that, in situations of high relevance, speakers are able to anticipate co-participants' actions and produce a response to that would-have-been co-participant's initiative action, and, by so doing, forestall it. For example, given a pre-sequence, speakers are able to anticipate the first pair part of the projected main sequence and produce the second pair part, thus forestalling the first pair part. Here is an example:

Extract 3.26 (Sinclair, 1976, cited in Levinson, 1983)

```
1. S: Have you got Embassy Gold please?
2. H: Yes dear (provides)
```

After she has confirmed the availability of Embassy Gold, H anticipates S to make an order and moves to attend to it even before the request is actually formulated, thus forestalling it. Also consider the following, where the mere mention of *Patriot Ledger* leads Bruce to anticipate the reason for the call and reject the invitation to subscribe to the paper even before it is made:

Extract 3.27 (Mey, 1993)

```
1. Telephone rings
2. Bruce     Hello
3. Caller:   Hello. I'm Julie from the Patriot Ledger.
             How are you today?
4. Bruce:    I'm fine thanks, but I already take two
             newspapers and I think a third one would be
             superfluous
```

In institutional talk, this possibility of anticipating and forestalling co-participants' initiative institutionally relevant action is relatively easy because institutional talk is task-oriented (Drew and Heritage, 1992).

Thus, after doctors' *howareyou*, the two interactional processes are deployed as follows: (1) patient, drawing on the standard shape as described above, anticipates and forestalls doctor's institutionally relevant next action, i.e. elicitation of a first concern; (2) patient pre-empts the on-going *howareyou* sequence. In turn, these actions lead to two possible outcomes, depending on the stage of the *howareyou* sequence at which pre-emption takes place. In some cases, pre-emption occurs very early on in the sequence, i.e. right after the utterance of *howareyou*, as in Extracts 3.2 and 3.18 above. In this case, I will speak of *early pre-emption*. As the two examples show, right after the doctor's *howareyou*, the patient reveals the reason for the visit. A third example of this possibility can be found in Extract 3.28 below.

Extract 3.28 (B0618)

```
1. D:  Come in ((door opens)) Hello
2. P:  Hello Dr {last name}
3. D:  Come and sit yourself down. ((door closes))
Right. How are you?
4. P:  ((laughs)) Er well I've got two things I've
       called to see you for today. One is my hands
       again. Erm
5. D:  Yeah
```

The second possibility, which I will refer to as *late pre-emption*, is for pre-emption to occur after the patient has provided a second pair part to the doctor's *howareyou*, usually in the form of a neutral response. As we have seen, after a neutral response, a closing third is a possible next action. In this case this next action is pre-empted and, along with it, other possible extensions of the sequence (reciprocal *howareyous* and same-action type series – see above). Examples of this second possibility are given in Extracts 3.21 and 3.22 above. Here is a third example.

Extract 3.29 (Gafaranga and Britten, 2005)

```
(Door opens)

1. D:  Hello Mr {last name}. How are you doing?
2. P:  Well- well not too bad really. I can still get
       these symptoms but I don't think they're- I
       don't know whether they're so bad [but
3. D:                                     [Mm
4. P:  I still get this blanching of the fa- it's
       round- it's round the mouth area you know (...)
```

Of course, patients may pre-empt the *howareyou* sequence in order to accomplish actions other than displaying the presenting concern. In this case, the presenting concern may come, without any further elicitation, after these intervening actions. Consider Extract 3.30 below. After the neutral response, the patient pre-empts the sequence and tells the doctor about X, the fieldworker who had been to see her for the pre-consultation interview. At the end of this narration, she directly moves into presenting the reason for her attendance at the surgery without any further elicitation.

Extract 3.30 (L0610C)

```
1. D:  Here we go. How are you?
2. P:  Er I'm all right thanks. Er {first name} came
       up on (0.2) last night. Last night
3. D:  Right
4. P:  And she's gonna come up next Wednesday
5. D:  [Right
6. P:  [No not last night. Wednesday night. Sorry.
       And she's coming up next Wednesday after I've
       been here. Right. The reason I er come to see
       you on the third of May I'm going away for a
       week. I'm- I'm going to erm Greece and er I
       got to thinking about my ears. And erm I-I- I
       panicked a bit to be honest (. . .)
```

To summarise, the aim of this section has been to elucidate the issue of how, in doctor–patient interaction, the doctor's *howareyou* is produced and understood as if it was a first concern elicitor while it 'does not, in and of itself, index patients' institutionally relevant concern' (Robinson, 2006: 39). In this section, I have demonstrated that, in doctor–patient interaction, the doctor's *howareyou* is basically the same as *howareyou* in ordinary everyday talk, and therefore the same as patients' own *howareyous*. In all three cases, *howareyou* is 'geared towards sociability rather than instrumental tasks' (Heritage and Clayman, 2010: 63). I have also identified and described two specific interactional practices that patients deploy in order to achieve talk which looks as if *howareyou* was a first concern elicitor. These are pre-emption, which allows them to shorten the *howareyou* sequence, and forestalling, which allows them to display their presenting concerns without waiting for the doctor to elicit them explicitly.

Thus the interaction between doctors' *howareyou* and the display of presenting concerns can take any of the four patterns shown in Figure 3.4. In the first pattern, the *howareyou* sequence is allowed to run its

---

i. Howareyou + concern elicitor + presenting concern
ii. Howareyou + late pre-emption + forestalling of concern elicitor + presenting concern
iii. Howareyou + early pre-emption + forestalling of concern elicitor + presenting concern
iv. No howareyou + concern elicitor + presenting concern

Figure 3.4   Four patterns in the use of *howareyou* in doctor–patient interaction

course in full, before a first concern elicitor is used to invite the patient to display their presenting concerns. This corresponds to what I have referred to above as the standard shape of the opening of the doctor–patient consultation. In the second pattern, the doctor's *howareyou* receives a second pair part, pre-emption takes place after the second pair part, i.e. at the level of the expansions and extensions of the *howareyou* sequence, and the doctor's first concern elicitor is forestalled. In the third, the second pair part of the *howareyou* sequence is pre-empted and the doctor's first concern elicitor is forestalled. Finally, in the fourth possibility, the *howareyou* sequence as a whole is pre-empted, the first concern elicitor occurring right after the exchange of greetings. It is in the second and third possibilities that *howareyou* looks as if it was a first concern elicitor, but these cannot be fully understood except with reference to the structure as a whole.

3.2.5   Accounting for structural diversity

As we have seen above, a standard shape for *howareyou* sequences in GP consultations exists. Yet variation from it is also common. How can this diversity be accounted for? How is it that the standard form is adopted only some of the time? Remember that, as demonstrated above, the various patterns result from the application of two different interactional processes: namely, pre-emption and forestalling. Therefore the question above can be rephrased as two separate ones: (1) why is it that the *howareyou* sequence is sometimes pre-empted; and (2) why is it that first concern elicitors are sometimes forestalled? The two questions are addressed in turn in the paragraphs below.

The answer to the first question starts from the by-now-well-established principle that talk is context-shaped (Drew and Heritage, 1992). In this respect, it is worth remembering, for example, that, as we have seen, *howareyou* sequences are routinely missing in emergency calls (Whalen and Zimmerman, 1987; Zimmerman, 1992). One reason for this shortening of the opening sequence is obviously the need to arrive at the reason for the call as quickly as possible. That is, the conversational structure reflects the emergency nature of the call (but see Heritage and Clayman, 2010: 62–3 for a more sophisticated discussion). As previously indicated, the data on which the *howareyou* sequence has been investigated come from general practice consultations. The institution of general practice, in the UK context at least, prides itself on its relational dimension. Because patients stay with the same doctor for a relatively long period of time, a lifetime in some cases, doctors and patients develop a relationship and get to know each other very well (Boddy, 1975; Thompson and Ciechanowski, 2003). In turn, it is believed that a good relationship positively affects the quality of the care patients receive. Thus, establishing a good doctor–patient rapport is felt to be an important communication skill for doctors to acquire (Silverman et al., 2005) and is even seen as an important phase of the consultation (e.g. Byrne and Long, 1976). Therefore, it is normal that this relational dimension of the institution of general practice is encoded in doctors' and patients' talk. For example, contrary to many other cases of institutional talk (Drew and Sorjen, 1997), as many of the extracts we have looked at show, doctors and patients often address each other as individuals, using their names rather than their institutional identities. In this respect, it is noteworthy that the institutional identity 'patient' is never used.

The use of *howareyou* can be understood as one of the practices through which participants show orientation to the relational dimension of general practice. As we have seen above, doctor-initiated *howareyou* is not different from its equivalent in everyday conversation. In everyday conversation, as Heritage and Clayman (2010: 63) say, *howareyou* is 'normally relevant for acquaintances who have a personal relationship grounded in shared biography'. Doctor-initiated *howareyous* can be understood along the same lines. As in ordinary everyday conversation, through the use of *howareyou*, participants accomplish relational work. In some cases, participants foreground this relational work and allow *howareyou* sequences to run their full course, thus producing the pattern '*howareyou* + first concern elicitor + presenting concern'. In some other cases, participants background relational work, at least this aspect of it, pre-empt the whole of the *howareyou* sequence and produce the pattern 'no *howareyou* + concern elicitor + presenting concern' (pattern 4). In between these two extremes, participants may touch on this relational aspect of talk, as if in passing, by opening the *howareyou* sequence and aborting it midway (pre-emption). Thus, if doctor-initiated *howareyou* is viewed in its institutional context, the four patterns fall along a

+*Howareyou* sequence	Late pre-emption	Early pre-emption	+*Howareyou* sequence

Figure 3.5   Fore- / back-grounding the relational dimension of general practice

continuum, corresponding to the degree to which the relational dimension of general practice is fore- / back-grounded, as in Figure 3.5.

As for the forestalling of doctors' first concern elicitors, I would like to suggest that it can be understood in terms of *doctorability* (Heritage and Robinson, 2006). Concerning this notion of doctorability, Heritage and Robinson write:

> At the beginning of the medical visit, the patients can face the task of presenting their medical concern as '*doctorable*'. For patients, a doctorable problem is one that is worthy of medical attention, worthy of counselling and, where necessary, medical treatment. (Heritage and Robinson, 2006: 54)

Heritage and Robinson discuss a number of verbal strategies patients use in presenting their problems as doctorable, including making diagnostic claims, invoking third parties and trouble resistance (2006: 65–83). Other researchers, notably Heath (2002), have shown that the same effect can be achieved non-verbally by 'demonstrating suffering'. Heath writes:

> Patients have to provide reasonable grounds for seeking medical help and, if necessary, gaining access to the sick role. (. . .) enactment and demonstrations not only allow us to give unique qualities to generic categories of mundane troubles, but they also help provide evidence of the difficulty and its severity in the particular case. (. . .) patients, through their enactments and demonstrations, underscore the uniqueness and severity of their complaints and provide good grounds for turning to the doctor. (. . .) in revealing their problems (through demonstrations), patients provide the doctor with an opportunity to see the very suffering incurred by the patient and the seriousness of the problem. (Heath, 2002: 613–14)

I would like to suggest that, by forestalling first concern elicitors, i.e. by skipping predictable steps of the standard shape, patients 'demonstrate' organisationally the urgency of their concerns and therefore their doctorability.

Briefly, three aspects of general practice explain the particular organisation of doctor-initiated *howareyou* sequences as I have detailed it in the last section. Firstly, general practice has a very important relational dimension. This aspect accounts for the fact that, in the data examined, doctors' *howareyou* is similar to *howareyou* in everyday conversation. In both cases, *howareyou* is 'geared towards sociability rather than instrumental tasks' (Heritage and Clayman, 2010: 63). Sometimes, sociability is fore-grounded, this leading to fully-fledged *howareyou* sequences, and it is back-grounded at some other times, this leading to the absence of such sequences. Secondly, the fact that general practice consultation, like any other instance of institutional talk, is goal-oriented militates against the use of *howareyou* sequences. A compromise between these two aspects of general practice is arrived at by pre-empting *howareyou* sequences: that is, by aborting them before they have run their course in full. Thirdly, the fact that, as in any other medical consultation, patients are faced with issues of doctorability and have to exhibit good grounds for seeing the doctor leads them to 'demonstrate' the urgency of their presenting concerns. They achieve this by forestalling doctors' first concern elicitors. All in all, in general practice consultations, doctor-initiated *howareyou* sequences are context-shaped, have an institutional character to themselves. The institution in which doctor-initiated *howareyou* sequences occur leaves its *fingerprint* on them.

3.2.6   Summary of the worked example

This discussion started from the observation that there is little agreement among researchers as to the nature of doctor-initiated *howareyou* in doctor–patient interaction. While some view it as a first concern elicitor in its own right, others maintain that it is not. Therefore two questions were raised: (1) is *howareyou* a first concern elicitor or is it not? (2) If it is not, how can the fact that it participates in sequences of talk which make it look as if it was a first concern elicitor be explained? To answer these questions, a corpus of general practice consultations collected in the Midlands and the South-east of England was examined. In examining these data, I adopted a comparative methodology as suggested by authors such as Drew and Heritage (1992) for the study of institutional talk.

Examination of this corpus of data allowed me to identify a number of reasons why doctors' *howareyou* should not be seen as a first concern elicitor. These are: (1) *howareyou* may co-occur with first concern elicitors without there being repair; (2) *howareyou* need not be responded to by displaying patient's presenting concerns; (3) non-medical responses to *howareyou* may co-occur with presenting concerns without there being repair; (4) *howareyou* does not occupy the same sequential position as first concern elicitors. In turn, this confirmation that doctor-initiated *howareyou* is not a first concern elicitor led to the issue of how *howareyou* appears in sequences which make it look like a first concern elicitor.

In addressing this issue, I demonstrated that situations where *howareyou* looks as if it was a first concern elicitor actually develop from the application of two interactional processes, namely pre-emption and forestalling. The first process allows patients to 'abort' the *howareyou* sequence before it runs its full course, while forestalling allows them to anticipate upcoming first concern elicitors and produce responses (presenting concerns) without any explicit elicitation. A combination of these two processes leads to two possible outcomes depending on the stage of the sequence where pre-emption takes place. In some cases, pre-emption takes place immediately after the doctor's *howareyou* (early pre-emption) and, in some other cases, it takes place after a second pair part has been provided to the doctor's *howareyou*. On this basis, a continuum of possibilities was observed. At one end of the continuum, we find situations where the *howareyou* sequence runs its full course and is followed by a first concern elicitor and presenting concerns. At the other end, we find situations where the *howareyou* sequence is completely absent but first concern elicitors are present. In between these two extremes, we find situations characterised by the pre-emption of the *howareyou* sequence and the forestalling of first concern elicitors. Finally, I went beyond structural description and accounted for the observed structural diversity. More specifically, having noted that there is a standard shape for *howareyou* sequences, I offered a functional explanation for deviations from it. On the one hand, I argued that *howareyou* sequences are pre-empted or not in order to back-ground or else fore-ground the relational dimension of general practice. On the other, I proposed that forestalling can be interpreted in terms of doctorability whereby patients anticipate and forestall doctors' first concern elicitors in order to demonstrate organisationally the urgency of their presenting concerns.

3.3 Discussion and conclusion

As indicated in the introduction, the purpose of this chapter has been to establish a methodology which can be used in approaching bilingualism as consisting of interactional practices. This methodology, it was maintained, should be inductive in nature and allow for an open exploration of data. The methodology, it was also asserted, should be applicable to both monolingual and bilingual practices. In concrete terms, the methodology was described as consisting of a number of specific actions that the researcher must accomplish, which actions can in turn be subdivided into two major categories, namely noticing a phenomenon / practice and pursuing it through an exploration of concrete data so as to come to grips with the issue of how the phenomenon or practice works. Since, as indicated above, the claim is that the methodology should apply for both monolingual and bilingual practices, this chapter has illustrated it by means of a monolingual interactional practice. The practice in question is the use of *howareyou* in doctor–patient interaction by way of eliciting patient's presenting concerns. The practice had been reported by many previous researchers and, in this case study, supplementary questions were asked: that is, whether *howareyou* is or is not a first concern elicitor; and if it is not, what interactional processes are deployed for it to look as if it were a first concern elicitor (step 1). To answer these questions, data were collected and explored indifferently, i.e. inductively. For example, instances of *howareyou* were examined independently of whether they led to the statement of presenting concerns or not. In turn, this allowed us to observe variation in the practice. Different patterns were observed (steps 2–5). Following this observation, a standard shape was identified, and a structural account (forestalling and pre-emption) was provided for non-standard patterns along with a functional explanation for their adoption (step 6). In the chapters that follow, the same methodological attitude is adopted in investigating interactional practices which involve the use of two or more languages.

Notes

1. Codes such as '(B0514C)' are used to locate individual consultations in the data set.
2. I have been given access to this data set within the context of a lectureship in concordance I held at the Department of Primary Care of the GKT School of Medicine in 2001–2, with funding from Sir Siegmund Voluntary Settlement. The data were collected in the context of an earlier study funded by the Department of Health as part of the Prescribing Research Initiative. Members of the study team were Nicky Britten, Nick Barber, Christine Barry, Colin Bradley and Fiona Stevenson.
3. I will use the form '*whatcanIdoforyou*' for exactly the same reason as I use '*howareyou*', i.e. to represent a type of concern elicitor and not necessarily the actual words used.

4 Language choice and speech representation in bilingual interaction

4.1 Introduction

The first bilingual practice we look at is language choice in speech representation in bilingual interaction. A number of scholars, including Gumperz (1982), Auer (1984, 1995), Alvarez-Caccamo (1998) and Alfonzetti (1998) and so on, have noticed that CS frequently occurs in the interactional site of speech representation, also often referred to as direct speech reporting (hereafter DSR).[1] However, despite these frequent sightings, no systematic account of the role of CS in DSR has actually been proposed. To be sure, some suggestions have been made, but none seems to be very satisfactory. On the one hand, scholars such as Gal (1979) and Myers-Scotton (1993b) adopt what is known as the *verbatim assumption* (Clark and Gerrig, 1990) and maintain that, in DSR, language choice is a mere reproduction of the medium of the 'original' utterance. Such a view is easily contradicted by the fact that, among bilingual speakers, the medium of DSR need not be the same as that of the original situation, assuming there indeed was an original situation. An alternative view, which may be termed the '*contextualisation assumption*' and is adopted by scholars such as Auer (1984, 1995), Alfonzetti (1998), Sebba and Wootton (1998) and so on, is that the role of language choice in DSR is to set 'off (. . .) reported speech against its surrounding conversational (often narrative) context' (Auer, 1995: 119) and therefore that the medium of DSR need not be the same as that of the original medium. It is in this sense that many of these authors use CS in DSR as evidence of the non-directionality of CS. In turn, this account faces a number of problems, including the fact that, in some cases at least, the direction of CS in DSR is meaningful. Therefore, the question of how language choice in DSR works remains entirely open. To address this issue, I begin by describing the diversity observed in DSR at the level of language choice.

4.2   Language choice patterns in direct speech reporting

Among bilingual speakers, an event, assuming there has been one, may be reported using its original medium. Extract 4.1 takes place among Rwandan friends and they are talking about political events in the period leading up to the 1994 political impasse and the ensuing genocide. In the extract, a speaker reports what some Rwandan politicians would have said and done. Given the Rwandan sociolinguistic context (Gafaranga, 1998), these politicians would have used Kinyarwanda–French language alternation as the medium. In reporting what they have said (highlighted), the same medium is used.

Extract 4.1

```
A:  X nawe ati non, ça ne peut pas marcher comme ça
    (.) Nawe avec sa faction baravuga bati pour com-
    mencer, bariya bantub'abadeputés, bariya batowe,
    ntuza ariya matora yabo turayanuye puisque ils se
    sont méconduits (.) à l'égard du parti ((laugh))
```

```
A:  X on his turn said no it can't work like that
    (.) he too with his group said to start with,
    those MPs, those elect MPs, those who have been
    elected, we invalidate those elections because
    they have misbehaved (.) towards the party
    ((laughter))
```

Language choice in Extract 4.2 below is another case where the medium of 'original' event is maintained in DSR. The context of this example is the invasion of Zaire (present day Democratic Republic of Congo) by the Rwandan army in 1996. At the time, many Rwandan refugees were camped in Eastern Congo, a region where Swahili is used as a lingua franca (Meeuwis and Blommaert, 1998). Participants in the conversation are saying that Zairians will blame the invasion of their country on these refugees and threaten to throw them out. In his contribution to the talk, participant A quotes Zairians and uses the language they plausibly could have used: namely, Swahili.

Extract 4.2

```
1. A:  ubu rero ab (.) buretse (.) abazayuruwa bagiye
       gutangira ngo (.) fukuza munyarwanda (.) [(  )
```

```
2. B:   [avec raison (.)[puisque turi imbwa
3. A:   [( ) ((laughter)) ariko
4. C:   avec raison (.) none se none wanzanira ibibazo
        iwanjye
```

```
1. A:   now Zairians Zair (.) wait a minute (.)
        Zairians are going to start saying kick out
        Rwandan(.) [(           )
2. B:   [rightly so (.) [as we do not deserve any
        respect
3. A:   [( ) ((laughter)) but
4. C:   rightly so (.) if you bring problems to my door
```

Alternatively, as Extract 4.3 shows, DSR may adopt a medium which could not have been used by the people quoted. In the example, participant A, a Rwandan in Belgium, is telling co-participants what happened to his family when they came to join him in Belgium. He is saying that, on arrival at the airport, they were asked a series of questions, including whether they were planning to go back and what type of tickets they were travelling on. Presumably, these questions were asked by Belgian immigration officials. As the transcript shows, in reporting the event, A uses Kinyarwanda. Clearly, it is unlikely that these immigration officials would actually have used Kinyarwanda.

Extract 4.3

```
1. A:   baki- bakigera ku kibuga rero aba baje
2. B:   nka wa mukobwa {first name} [we rwose
3. A:   [mbakubise mu modoka tugiye mu rugo
(long talk omitted)
4. A:   atubwira ibibazo bari bagize kuko barahageze
        bakabaza (.) ngo ese ngo ese muje muzasubirayo
        (.) ngo mufite amatickets yahe (.) [aba barit-
        uramira nyine
5. C:   [umh
```

```
1. A:   when they arrived at the airport when they came
2. B:   like that girl {fist name} [as for her
3. A:   [I put them in the car to go home
(long talk omitted)
4. A:   he told us the problem they had had for when
        they arrived they were asked are you going to
```

> **go back (.) what kind of tickets do you have**
> **(.)** [these of course kept quiet
> 5. C: [umh

A similar situation is found in Extract 4.4 below. In the conversation, participants are talking about the racism they face in the different countries where they live. A, who lives in Germany, sees racism in the kinds of question Germans ask overseas students, including himself. He quotes them as asking, among other things, 'Are you studying here to go back and work in your country?'. As the transcript shows, this question uses French as its medium while its plausible original medium is German.

Extract 4.4

1. A: ikikwereka ukuntu ari ntuza ari- badashaka
      abanyamahanga iwabo (.) baraza bakakubaza (.)
      urikwiga iki ah ngo ***c'est pour aller travail-***
      ler dans ton pays? ((laughter))
2. B: *il faut* kubasubiza uti ***oui***
3. A: reka jye ndababwira nti ubungubu nta muntu
      nti- jye ndababwira- jyewe ndabibabwira
      nti (.) *la situation* yo mu Rwanda ni *cata-*
      strophique nta muntu ushobara gu gu gu*planifi*a
      (.) ubu (.) aho azaba ari

----

1. A: what shows you that they are - that they don't
      want foreigners is that they come and ask you
      (.) what are you studying ah say ***is it to go***
      and work in your country? ((laughter))
2. B: *you should* tell them yes
3. A: no (.) I tell them today nobody- as for me I
      tell them- I tell them (.) *the situation* in
      Rwanda is *catastrophic* nobody can *plan* (.)
      today (.) where they will be

The extent of the diversity in language choice in the interactional site of DSR can begin to be grasped if one looks at Figure 4.1, resulting from a survey of language choice in DSR in a corpus of bilingual conversations among the Rwandans in Belgium (Gafaranga, 1998). Three observations can be made, based on this table: (1) Kinyarwanda–French language alternation can be used independently of the medium of 'original' talk. Sometimes, this is as a result of changing the medium of original talk. (2) The medium of 'original' talk may be maintained in

'Original' talk	Language alternation	Kinyarwanda	French	Other
Direct speech reporting				
Language alternation	X	X	X	X
Kinyarwanda		X		
French			X	X
Other				X

Top row: medium of 'original' talk; left-hand column: medium of direct speech reporting; X: actual choice observed in the data.

Figure 4.1   Language choice and direct speech reporting among bilingual Rwandans in Belgium (Gafaranga, 1998: 283)

DSR. (3) French may be used even when the 'original' medium was not French. In other words, if the medium of 'original' talk is changed, this change may be in the direction of Kinyarwanda–French language alternation or in that of French. Therefore, an account of language choice in the practice of speech representation in this corpus of data should account for all these possibilities. The sections below account for these possibilities observed in the corpus of bilingual conversations among Rwandans in Belgium by way of illustrating how language choice in DSR reporting works in bilingual conversation in general – that is, by way of illustrating how bilingualism, at this level of DSR – can be viewed as an interactional practice.

4.3   Towards an account of language choice in speech representation

4.3.1   Direct speech reporting as demonstration

As an aspect of language use, DSR has been studied from a variety of perspectives (linguistics, literary criticism, sociology, philosophy, etc.) and it is not my intention to review this literature here (see Holt, 1996; Thompson, 1996; Baynham, 1996; Myers, 1991; Clift and Holt, 2007, etc.). Rather, I intend to pick up one theory, Clark and Gerrig's (1990) *demonstration theory*, and use it as a starting point to explore the data at hand and, by so doing, propose an account of the practice in general. Clark and Gerrig's starting point is the rejection of what they call the *verbatim assumption*, namely the assumption that DSR is a mere verbatim reproduction of an original utterance (Baynham, 1996: 64). Rather, to use Tannen's words, they see DSR as primarily a creation of the speaker rather than the party quoted (Tannen, 1989: 99). Indeed, in line with Clark and Gerrig, Tannen (1989) speaks of 'constructed dialogue' to highlight the nature of reported speech as a local accomplishment rather than a verbatim reproduction of previous talk. Clark and Gerrig discuss many reasons why the verbatim assumption must be rejected, but space does not allow me to go into the detail of their argument. Three pieces of evidence, just to mention these, why DSR should be seen as a local interactional accomplishment are: speakers sometimes report events which they themselves signal as yet to come; sometimes they only report 'community voices' (Thompson, 1996) rather than specific events; and, in some cases, only thought rather than previous talk, is reported (Haakana, 2007). By way of an illustration, consider Extract 4.2 above. As the transcript shows, the event reported is yet to take place. Zairians are yet to say 'Fukuza munyarwanda'. That is, there has not been any previous interaction for participants to report. Likewise, in Extracts 4.3 and 4.4, categories (community voices), rather than specific speakers, are reported. It is for this reason that the term 'speech representation', rather than 'direct speech reporting', is felt to be a more appropriate label for the practice (see the title of this chapter).

Secondly, Clark and Gerrig's demonstration theory draws on Peirce's division of signs into indices, symbols and icons. Thus, their theory is based on the view that, in face-to-face communication, there are three fundamental methods of conveying information: indicating, describing and demonstrating (1990: 765). To clarify the differences between these methods, Clark and Gerrig use, among other examples, the one of 'George limps'. The information that George limps can be communicated through description by uttering the sentence: 'George limps'. In this case, communication is essentially a mental activity of associating what is said and what is meant. There is no experience, direct or indirect, of the situation described. The same meaning can be communicated, through indication, by pointing at George while he is walking, such that the interlocutor actually sees George limping. Here, communication consists of direct perceptual experience (Clark and Gerrig, 1990: 767). Finally, the same meaning can be communicated, through a demonstration, by imitating some of George's body movements. In this case, the hope is that the interlocutor will be able 'to experience *what it is like* to perceive the things depicted' (1990: 765; my emphasis), what it is like to see George limping.

According to Clark and Gerrig, the two main properties of demonstrations are that they are *non-serious actions* and that they are *partial and selective*. The term 'non-serious action' is borrowed from Goffman (1974), according to whom non-serious actions are 'transformations' of serious actions. Serious actions are 'real and actual', while non-serious actions are neither real nor actual and need to refer to their serious counterpart for meaning. For example, right now, I am really and actually typing on my computer. This is a serious action. Later on in the evening, I might mimic what I am doing right now – for example, move my fingers – by way of telling my children what I have been doing all day. While mimicking, I will not be really and actually typing on the computer. This is a non-serious action. As non-serious actions, demonstrations relate to serious actions in three ways: (1) demonstrations are performed as part of serious activities – that is, they have a specific function to serve within the context of the serious activity. For instance, in the example above, the typing demonstration would be performed as part of the telling of my day. (2) Demonstrations must be distinguished from serious actions they are part of, that is, their boundaries – their beginnings and ends – must be clear. And (3) demonstrations are either 'component parts' of the serious activity or they are 'concurrent' with the serious activity (Clark and Gerrig, 1990: 766). For instance, in the same typing example above, I might say 'I spent the day doing this' and then do the demonstration (move my fingers). In this case, the demonstration is said to be a component part of the serious activity of telling my children what I spent the day doing. Alternatively, I might say 'I spent the day typing on the computer' and, while saying this, do the demonstration. In this case, the demonstration is concurrent with the serious activity.

On the other hand, demonstrations are partial and selective in the sense that, in a demonstration, not every aspect of the depicted action is enacted. Take the serious action of typing on the computer. This action includes acts such as movement of fingers, movement of the eyes, reading of the screen, breaks to think what to do next and so on. In the non-serious action, not all of these will be enacted and the one act which will be enacted – for example, movement of fingers – might have to be exaggerated in order actually to convey the intended meaning. Following from the fact that demonstrations are partial and selective, Clark and Gerrig identify four possible aspects to every demonstration: (1) depictive aspects, (2) supportive aspects, (3) annotative aspects and (4) incidental aspects. A depictive aspect is any one that has been chosen to represent the action depicted. In the typing example, the depictive aspect is the movement of fingers. Supportive aspects are those which are necessary for the depictive aspect to be possible. For instance, in the typing demonstration, for the movement of fingers to be possible as depictive of the action of typing on the computer, the arms must be in a certain position (flexed at the level of the elbow). Thirdly, annotative actions are those which are added as a commentary on what is being demonstrated (1990: 768). For example, while demonstrating typing, I might produce noises imitating the ones produced by hitting keys on the keyboard. Finally, incidental aspects are those which, although part of the action being demonstrated, are completely ignored in the demonstration. For example, the fact that, while actually typing, I am in a seated position might be completely ignored in the demonstration. Clearly, of the four, the most important is the depictive aspect.

Drawing on the ideas above, Clark and Gerrig argue that 'prototypical quotation is a demonstration of what a person did in saying something (. . .) (and that) quotations (. . .) display all the properties of genuine demonstrations' (1990: 769). As we have seen, the first property of demonstrations is that they are non-serious actions. To see that direct speech reports are non-serious actions, consider Extract 4.3 above. As we have seen, the reports in the example are questions as to whether A's family were planning to go back and what type of tickets they were travelling on. Clearly, in uttering these questions, A is not really and actually asking them. Likewise, in 4.2, A is not really and actually threatening to kick out Rwandans. In either case, A's actions are only 'patterned on' or 'transformations of' serious actions which are already meaningful in terms of some primary framework (1990: 770). Secondly, the quotations are performed as part of serious activities: namely, the narration of what happened to A's family when they came to join him in Belgium (Extract 4.3) and the narration of the anticipated reaction by Zairians to the Rwandan invasion (Extract 4.2). Thirdly, in both cases, reports are clearly set apart from surrounding conversational contexts by the use of an introductory component (Holt, 2007) ('bakabaza' in 4.3 and 'bagiye gutangira' in 4.2), the use of the direct speech report marker 'ngo' in both cases, and slight pauses (.) before and after the quotations. Finally, both cases are instances of concurrent demonstrations since they do not lead to any suspension of the serious activities.

The second property of demonstrations is that they are partial and selective. Regarding this property, Clark and Gerrig write:

> Face to face, people can demonstrate many things. When Alice demonstrates for Ben what George said, she can easily depict the words he uttered. But using her voice, face, arms, and body, she can also help depict George's language, dialect, drunkenness, indignation, hesitancy, arrogance, flamboyance, stuffy manner, and a variety of other things. What she chooses to depict depends on the experience she wants Ben to have. (1990: 775)

Elsewhere, they write that 'speakers can quote anything they can recognizably demonstrate, from intonation and dialect to non-linguistic actions of all sorts' (1990: 782). However, all these possibilities can be grouped under three general categories (1990: 775):

1. delivery: voice pitch (male, female, child), voice age (adult, child, oldster), voice quality (raspy, nasal, slurred), speech defects (lisp, stutter), emotional states (anger, sarcasm, excitement) and so on.
2. language: language proper (English, Dutch, Japanese), dialect (British English, Bostonian English, Scottish)
3. linguistic acts: illocutionary act (question, promise, request), propositional expression (content), locutionary act (the sentence uttered), utterance act (the utterance issued with repairs and so on).

Thus, in Extract 4.5, delivery is the depictive aspect. Talk is about the language situation in Belgium and participants are saying that it can lead to very heated debates. In his contribution, A portrays this situation by means of DSR. As the transcript shows, the quotation is organised in short chunks of words with many direct speech markers ('ngo') and many recycles, with the purpose of conveying specific emotional states, namely heated debate. As a result, the content of what is being said serves only as a supporting aspect. As for the medium of the 'original' event (either French or Flemish), it is incidental.

Extract 4.5

1. A: si byo by' ino aha ino ahangaha (.) hari
      ibintu bita *les compétences linguistiques*
2. B: umh
3. A: ibyo bya *compétences linguistiques* nibyo wumva
      bari gutukanaho ngoo ngo ngo **bourgmestre** ngo
      utegeka aha n' aha ngo **chez les** *flamands* ngo
      ntabwo azi (.) **igi***flamand* ngo **avuga gake** ngo
      niyo umu- ngo **niyo umukecuru w' umu***flamand* ngo
      agiye ku- kuvugana na *bourgmestre* ngo **yumva**
      ari ku- atari kucyumva ngo **atari kumwumva**
      ngo *comme il faut* (.) **umh uwo mu***bourgmestre*
      niba baramutoraguye (.) **niba** uretse ko bitan-
      ashoboka ngo abe ari nk'umu*wallon*

----

1. A: like things here (.) they have things they
      call *linguistic competencies*

2. B: umh
3. A: those *linguistic competencies* you hear people
        quarrelling about them saying **the mayor** saying
        who is in charge of here saying **in a Flemish-**
        speaking area saying **he / she doesn't know** (.)
        Flemish saying **when a** saying **when an old woman**
        who is Flemish saying **when she goes to talk**
        to the mayor saying **she finds that he / she's**
        not understanding it saying **he / she's under-**
        standing her saying **as he / she should** (.) umh
        if that mayor has been picked up (from the
        street) (.) except that it's not possible for
        him / her to be *Walloon*

Also consider Extract 4.6. Speaker A, a Rwandan priest, is saying that his parishioners take charge of the different aspects of life in the parish. He illustrates this using the example of the choir, saying that, on Sundays, when the clock strikes 10:30 am, the choir starts singing whether he asks them to do so or not.

Extract 4.6

1. A: saa ine n'igice (.) mu kadomo (.) inanga ihita
        ivuga (.) kuko baba batangiye
2. B: ((laughter))
3. A: naba nkivugana n'umuntu *dans [le fond* ()
4. B: [ubwo baba batangiye
(two turns omitted)
5. A: misa itangira saa ine n'igice (.) saa ine
        n'igice *top* rero **umhoooooooooo** (.) *chant*
        d'entrée
6. B: umh
7. A: nkaba *obligé* yo kurekura uwo muntu

----

1. A: at half past ten (.) to the minute (.) instru-
        ments start playing (.) for they are starting
2. B: ((laughter))
3. A: whether I am still speaking to somebody *in*
        [the back ( )
4. B: [they start
(two turns omitted)
5. A: the mass starts at half past ten (.) at half

```
           past ten sharp (.) umhoooooooooo (.) the entry
           song
6. B:      umh
7. A:      then I have to leave the person I was speaking
           to
```

This is a case of quotation as component demonstration because, during the performance of the quotation, the description is suspended and is resumed after it. In this quotation, the depictive aspect is delivery (singing) and everything else, including content and language, is incidental.

If, as indicated above, speakers can quote anything (Clark and Gerrig, 1990: 775), a question arises as to how they decide what to quote and whether their choices are random or orderly. To begin to address this issue, we note that, as Clark and Gerrig argue, quotations are non-serious actions, consist of frame shift from the primary frame that we take to be immediate reality, to another frame shared for the purposes of the interaction (Myers, 1991: 379). In other words, and in ethnomethodological terms, DSR is a case of functional deviance. Two general functions are identified: namely, *detachment* and *direct experience*. By detachment, Clark and Gerrig mean the fact that, in using DSR, the speaker takes responsibility only for *presenting* the quoted matter, the responsibility for the depicted aspects themselves remaining with the source speaker (1990: 792). In Goffman's (1981) words, the speaker is only an animator. As for direct experience, Clark and Gerrig mean the fact that we perceive the depicted aspects partly as we would the aspects they are intended to depict (1990: 791). For example, the function of quotation in Extract 4.6 above is direct experience. In the example, it is as if A's addressees are being asked to experience the singing themselves. On the other hand, Extract 4.2 is a case of detachment for solidarity purposes. DSR serves solidarity purposes when, through it, participants assert 'I am demonstrating something we both can interpret correctly' (1990: 793). In this example, quotation works effectively only because all participants can recognise that it is meant to elicit laughter. Unlike in Extract 4.6, here participants are not being asked to experience the threat themselves. However, as Myers (1991: 379) says, in any quotation, there are elements of direct experience and of detachment.

Thus the decision as to which aspect to report, rather than being random, is functional. In actual situations, speakers choose to depict any aspect which can best serve the intended function. In Extract 4.5 above, for instance, the intended function is that of direct experience. Addressees are being invited to experience the intensity of the debates regarding bilingualism in Belgium. To achieve this function, A chooses to depict delivery, content serving as a supportive element while language choice is incidental. Also consider Extract 4.7 below. Participants in the interaction are saying that some Rwandans' pronunciation of French has been strongly influenced by Kinyarwanda. To illustrate this, A uses the example of a bishop who, he says, came to give a talk at his school. The specific aspect of the 'original' event he decides to depict, with a view to allowing other participants to experience the bishop's pronunciation of French, is the cluster [nt]. In French, [t] is dental occlusive and remains such in the context of the nasal [n]. In Kinyarwanda, on the other hand, in contact with [n], [t] moves back to the ridge and ceases to be occlusive as a stream of air is allowed to go out through the nose. Thus, in the example, A reports the sentence 'Le roi Rwabugiri a été interonisé dans les montagnes de Ntongwe,' stressing the cluster [nt]. In this case, pronunciation of this cluster is the depictive aspect, everything else including content, becoming secondary.

Extract 4.7

```
1. A:    hari um- umusenyeri witwaga {first name}
         yigeze kuza kuduha conférence (.) à l'école
         cyera niga muri secondaire (.) araatubwira
         ngo (.) le roi Rwabugiri a été interonisé
         dans les montagnes de ntongwe ((laughter))
2. A&B   ((laughter))
3. A:    ugash- ugashakisha niba ari igifaransa arimo
         avuga cyangwa niba ari ikinyarwanda
4. C:    S ndamuzi
5. A:    ngo il a été interonisé [((laughter))
6. B:                            [interonisé
7. A:    dans les montagnes ((laughter))
```

```
1. A:    One bishop called {first name} one day came
         to give a talk at our school when I was
         still at secondary school and (.) he said
         King Rwabugiri was enthroned in the hills of
         Ntongwe ((laughter))
2. B:    ((laughter))
3. A:    and you'd wonder whether he was speaking
         French or Kinyarwanda
4. A&B:  ((laughter))
5. C:    I know S
```

```
6. A:    he was enthroned ((laughter))
7. B:    enthroned
8. A:    in the hills ((laughter))
```

To summarise, DSR must be understood as a demonstration because it has the two main aspects of any demonstration: namely, being a selective and non-serious action. DSR is a non-serious action for it corresponds to what Goffman (1974) calls frame shift at various levels or footings. As a shift of frame, DSR is necessarily functional. As we have seen, the functions of DSR can be thought of either in terms of detachment or in terms of direct experience. On the other hand, DSR is selective and partial because it depicts some aspects of the event reported and disregards some others. The selection itself of which aspect to depict depends on the intended function. Once an aspect of the event reported has been selected, other aspects work either as supportive elements or as annotative elements. Alternatively, they may simply be incidental. I propose that the issue of how language choice in DSR works can be solved in the light of this general theory of quotations as demonstrations.

4.3.2   Language choice as the depictive element

As we have seen, some of the questions that language choice in the interactional site of DSR raises are: why is it that DSR is sometimes found to adopt the medium of 'original' event and to change it some other times? If the medium of 'original' event is not retained, what does it change into and why? In order to be able to address these questions, a respecification is necessary. As Clark and Gerrig argue, DSR is not a mere reproduction of a previous event. Rather, DSR must be seen as the creation of the current speaker. That is to say, both questions above are based on a verbatim assumption, an assumption which, as we have seen, is questionable. If the verbatim assumption is rejected, the valid question to ask becomes: why is it that, in speech representation, speakers sometimes stay within the current medium and depart from it some other times? That is, current medium, rather than 'original' medium, must be seen as the point of reference. Thus, given two examples such as Extract 4.2 and Extract 4.3, the question to ask is: why is it that, in 4.3, Kinyarwanda–French language alternation – that is, the medium of current conversation – is adopted in doing DSR and why is it that it is deviated from in Extract 4.2? It is also why, in Extract 4.2, deviance from the medium takes the specific direction of Swahili, for it could have gone in the direction of French, as in Extract 4.4. Indeed, why does deviance take the direction of French in Extract 4.4?

Two initial situations may be observed. As Clark and Gerrig (1990) have noted, in DSR, language (choice) itself may be depictive, but it may also be incidental. If language choice is incidental, the default choice, i.e. current medium, is adopted. In turn, this is understandable because, as argued in Gafaranga (2007b), the medium is a norm, deviance from which must be accountable. Conversely, if language choice itself is the depictive aspect in DSR, 'original' medium must be used. Elsewhere, I have spoken of the contrast *medium reporting* versus *content reporting* (1998), but this is a very gross simplification, as we will see shortly. An example of language choice as a depictive aspect can be found in Extract 4.7 above. As we have seen, the function of DSR in this instance can be characterised as direct experience. The aim is to have co-participants experience the reported speaker's way of pronouncing French. Obviously, the only way this could be achieved is by medium reporting, by using the medium of original talk and, even then, selecting specific aspects of it to emphasise, namely the pronunciation of the cluster [nt]. Another example of medium reporting is Extract 4.8 below, an extension of Extract 4.3. As we have seen, A is narrating an event which happened to his family when they came to join him in Brussels. The on-going topic, which occasions the story, is that children are losing competence in Kinyarwanda. A narrates a story illustrating this. He says that, after his family had cleared customs, he took them in his car and they told him what had happened to them. In addition to the family, present in the car was a Belgian friend who had offered to help A pick up his family from the airport. Because of the presence of this non-Kinyarwanda speaker, French had been adopted as the medium, leading the child to complain about this choice of a language he did not understand and to threaten that, if they did not stop, he too would speak 'Zairian' (Swahili). In this case, the choice of Swahili in the highlighted quotation is meant to illustrate this use of 'Zairian' by the child, i.e. to bring co-participants to experience directly the child's use of 'Zairian'. As in Extract 4.7, discussed above, the content of what is reported to have been said is incidental.

Extract 4.8

```
1. A:   baki- bakigera ku kibuga rero aba baje
2. B:   nka wa mukobwa {first name} [we rwose
3. A:              [mbakubise mu modoka tugiye mu rugo (. . .)
        atubwira ibibazo bari bagize kuko barahageze
        bakabaza (.) ngo ese ngo ese muje muzasubi-
        rayo (.) ngo mufite amatickets yahe (.) [aba
        barituramira nyine
4. C:                                            [umh
```

```
5. A:    noneho umwana aratubwira (.) ati ubu mvuye
         muri Zaire (.) ati murakomeza kuvuga ibyo
         bifaransa nanjye ndavuga [ikizayiruwa
         ((laughter))
6. C:    [ndavuga ikizayiruwa ((laughter))
7. A:    ati Habari gani? ((laughter))
8. B&D:  ((laughter))
```

```
1. A:    when they arrived at the airport when they
         came
2. B:    like that girl {first name} [as for her
3. A:    [I put them in the car to go home (...) he
         told us the problem they had had for when
         they arrived they were asked are you going
         to go back (.) what kind of tickets do you
         have (.) [these of course kept quiet
4. C:    [umh
5. A:    and then the child told us (.) I am coming
         from Zaire (.) he said if you keep on speak-
         ing French [I will speak Zairian ((laughter))
6. C:    [I will speak Zairian ((laughter))
7. A:    he said How are you? ((laughter))
8. B&D:  ((laughter))
```

As for the situation where language choice is incidental, the first possibility is when content is reported. Consider Extract 4.3 again (part of
Extract 4.8 above). As we have seen, the aim of reporting is to give some
examples of the questions A's family were asked when they arrived at
Zaventem airport. That is to say, A is reporting the content of what
was said, and how it was said is felt to be irrelevant. As a consequence,
Kinyarwanda–French language alternation is adopted, even though it
could not possibly have been used in the 'original' event. Likewise, consider Extract 4.9 below. A is saying that he has nice, friendly neighbours.
By way of illustrating this, likening his neighbourhood to the Rwandan
countryside, he says that they invite him for drinks and even for food.
To make his narrative more vivid, he uses the strategy of speech representation, phrasing the invitations as they would be by the neighbours.
Here again, because the medium these invitations actually take is
incidental, A uses current medium, namely Kinyarwanda – French language alternation, even though the Belgian neighbours cannot possibly
use this language variety.

Extract 4.9

1. A: barantumira- akan*telephon*a ati **yayaya** (.) ni
      nk'iwacu mu giturage (.) ati **nabonye akadivayi**
      wanyarutse tukagasogongera tukumva uko kameze
2. B: *c'est vrai?*
3. A: eeh [((laughter))
4. B: [((laughter))
5. A: abenshi b'ahangaha benshi ni abahinzi (unclear)
6. B: umh
7. A: ati **irukanka twakoze bya**sauc*issons-* **yewe waje**
      tukabyumva niba biryoshye?

----

1. A: they invite me- they *call* and says **yayaya** (.)
      it's like home in the countryside (.) says **I**
      have a small wine come and have a taste
2. B: *really?*
3. A: eeh [((laughter))
4. B: [((laughter))
5. A: most people around here are farmers (unclear)
6. B: umh
7. A: says **come quick we've made** *sausages-* **let's**
      taste them and see if they are nice

However, content need not be the depictive aspect for current medium to be adopted. In Extract 4.5, for example, we have seen that delivery, that is the use of short utterances as if many people were talking at the same time, is the depictive element. The aim of DSR is to depict the reported debate as heated. Consequently, as the actual medium of the debates is irrelevant, Kinyarwanda–French language alternation, the default choice for current interaction, is used. Thus, rather than the contrast content versus medium reporting, a more realistic contrast appears to be [+*medium reporting*] versus [–*medium reporting*].

4.3.3 *Language choice as a supportive element*

As the discussion above shows, in DSR, language choice can be depictive, just as it may be incidental. A third possibility is for it to be used as a supportive element. In this case, without being the focus of direct speech as such, language choice either adds new meaning to what is being said or reinforces it in various ways. Consider Extract 4.2

again. In this example, content is relevant. Therefore, we can speak
of content reporting. However, language choice is also relevant. To
understand the function of language choice in this example, I propose
we start by observing that there is a feeling of dissociation between
Zairians and Rwandan refugees, including participants in this interaction (us versus them). These categories are associated with two different
ways of speaking. Current participants use Kinyarwanda–French language alternation; Zairians use a different medium. Elsewhere, I have
spoken of language preference as a membership categorisation device
(Gafaranga, 2001; Torras and Gafaranga, 2002). By enacting these linguistic identities, the speaker is able to evoke further category-bound
features, further meanings associated with being Zairian, including that
of laughable people. In this sense, language choice can be said to be used
metaphorically (Blom and Gumperz, 1972; Gumperz, 1982). In other
words, language choice is used as a supportive element, as an additional
resource, even though it is not itself the primary focus of DSR.

Also consider Extract 4.10 below. In this episode, participants are
saying that it is not good to live in the countryside for one is easily identified as different. In the example, two stories are used by way of exempli-
fying this. In the course of the narratives, DSR occurs. As in Extract 4.4,
here the main focus is on what was said (content). However, here too,
two categories of people are involved, namely current participants (and
their Rwandan friends) and the people reported, white Belgians. In both
cases, the thrust of the talk is such that current participants have to distance themselves from the people whose talk they are reporting. In both
cases, this identity contrast is reflected at the level of language choice,
with current participants using Kinyarwanda–French language alternation while the white community is attributed the use of French.

Extract 4.10

1. A: nagiye kumusura (.) nsigaje kilometero nk'
       icumi ngo ngere iwe (.) uwo mbajije wese (.)
       ngo ah ngo *tu vas chez monsieur* (.) *le mon-
       sieur là le noir*
2. B: ((laughter))
3. A: umh *tu t'imagines* ngo *tu vas chez le monsieur
       là* (.) *le monsieur le noir*
4. C: eh *donc* bose bamuzi
(. . .)
5. B: *oui* ejobundi nagiye mu nama ya {first name} (.)
       ejobundi *dimanche*
6. C: umh

```
7. B:   numva abantu bari kumbwira S utuye {first name}
        muri région- muri région ya {name omitted} (.)
        [bamuzi
8. A:   [c'est ça
9. B:   twari mu nama gutya noneho ikizungu kiba
        kirambwiye ngo (.) donc tu es Rwandais (.)
        il y a un Rwandais qui habite dans la mairie
        {first name} dans trente kilomètres ngo il
        était militaire
```

```
1. A:   I went to visit him (.) about ten kilome-
        tres before I got to his place (.) everybody
        I asked would say you are going to see mister
        (.) mister the black
2. B:   ((laughter))
3. A:   umh can you imagine say you are going to see
        mister (.) mister the black
4. C:   eh so everybody knows him
(talk omitted)
5. B:   yes two days ago I went to the meeting of
        {first name} (.) two days ago on Sunday
6. C:   umh
7. B:   I heard people telling me about S who lives
        {first name} in the district of {first name} (.)
        [they knew him
8. A:   [that's it
9. B:   we were sitting like this in a meeting and a
        white man told me (.) so you are Rwandan there
        is a Rwandan who lives {first name} (.) thirty
        kilometres from here (.) he said he was in the
        army (.)
```

It is at this level of language choice as a supportive aspect in DSR that the issues of whether to retain 'original' medium or not and, if not, what to change it into, arise. And they arise precisely because both content and language choice are relevant. That is to say, the issue arises because DSR is of the 'component part' type. Because language choice is relevant, as in the case of medium reporting, ideally, 'original' medium will be retained. On the other hand, because content is relevant, language choice in DSR must take account of participants' competence-related language preference (Torras and Gafaranga, 2002).

Thus, when language preference is not an issue, 'original' medium is retained, as in Extract 4.2 above. As we have seen, among Rwandans, Zairians are associated with Swahili. In addition, current participants, just like any Rwandans, are competent enough in Swahili to be able to understand the meaning of 'fukuza munyarwanda' (kick out the Rwandan). However, the same cannot be said of the choice of French in Extract 4.10 above. It is not the case that, for Rwandans in Belgium, all Belgians speak French. How do we explain this choice of French?

One possible answer could be that French was actually used as the medium in the 'original' event. However, this answer has to be rejected on two grounds. Firstly, the answer unjustifiably subscribes to the verbatim assumption, as the 'original' interaction could actually have taken place in Flemish. Secondly, such an answer is falsified by instances of language choice in DSR, as illustrated in Extract 4.4 (reproduced below as 4.11 for convenience).

Extract 4.11

1. A: ikikwereka ukuntu ari ntuza- ari- badashaka
abanyamahanga iwabo (.) baraza bakakubaza (.)
urikwiga iki? ah ngo *c'est pour aller travail-*
ler dans ton pays? ((laughter))
2. B: *il faut* kubasubiza uti *oui*
3. A: reka jye ndababwira nti **ubungubu nta muntu-**
nti- jye ndababwira- jyewe ndabibabwira
nti (.) *la situation* yo mu **Rwanda ni cata-**
strophique nta muntu ushobara gu gu gu*planifi*a
(.) **ubu (.) aho azaba ari**

----

1. A: what shows you that they are- that they don't
want foreigners is that they come and ask you
(.) **what are you studying** ah say *is it to go*
and work in your country? ((laughter))
2. B: *you should* tell them *yes*
3. A: no (.) I tell them **today nobody-** as for me I
tell them- I tell them (.) *the situation* in
Rwanda is *catastrophic* nobody can *plan* (.)
today (.) where they will be

As we have seen, participants in the conversation are talking about the racism they suffer in the different countries where they live. Participant A, who lives in Germany, illustrates this by saying that a typical question Germans ask foreign students is whether they will go back to their countries. In the example, three interesting situations can be observed. On the one hand, the native Germans are reported to ask two questions typically: namely, 'uri kwiga iki?' (what are you studying?) and 'c'est pour travailler dans ton pays?' (is it to go and work in your country?). As it can be seen, one of the questions uses the medium of Kinyarwanda, while the other uses the medium of French. Obviously, the reported speakers could not have used either of these two languages. On the other hand, the report consists of a dialogue in which A himself typically becomes involved. Again, as can be seen, while one of the questions that the Germans are typically said to ask is in French, A's answers are reported in Kinyarwanda–French language alternation, the medium of current interaction, as if 'original' talk had taken place in what Gafaranga and Torras (2001) refer to as the parallel mode. Finally, it is important to note that, in the report, content is important and the report is of the component part type.

In order for all three situations to be accounted for, the choice of French to report the second question must be seen as a case of language choice as a supportive element. On the one hand, the choice of French allows the speaker to contrast the two questions: the question which is neutral (question 1), which serves as a context (Rae and Kerby, 2007), and the focal question, which denotes racism on the part of the people reported (question 2). By deviating from the medium, A is able to highlight the second question. This is a case of what Chan (2004) calls 'textualisation'. On the other hand, the contrast between the choice of French to report the Germans' talk and that of Kinyarwanda to report current speaker's own talk corresponds to the social categories 'racists' and 'victims', which underlie the on-going talk. Through language choice, A is able to distance himself from the Germans, whom he is affirming to be racist. As in Extract 4.2, all of the above could have been achieved by using German, presumably the medium of 'original' interaction. However, participant B (myself) does not speak German. The choice of German would have hindered communication of content. Therefore, it is safe to say that French was adopted, not because it was used in the 'original' event, but rather as a compromise strategy, allowing the speaker to highlight the above contrasts while, at the same time, attending to the relevance of content. And, if this analysis of language choice in Extract 4.11 is accepted, a similar account can be proposed for language choice in Extract 4.10 as well. In Extract 4.10, French would have been chosen, not necessarily because it was the medium of 'original' talk, but rather because it allowed participants both to attend to content and to distance themselves from the people they are reporting. In short, language choice in DSR is neither a mere matter of reproducing the medium of 'original' talk nor that of contrasting the reported material and the surrounding interactional context. Rather, it is a question of whether language choice itself is being reported or not, and, if it is, whether language choice itself is the depictive aspect or whether it is a supportive aspect. And in the latter case, it is a matter of whether or not it runs across participants' competence-related language preference.

4.4 Conclusion

In Chapter 3, a methodology for investigating bilingualism as consisting of various interactional practices was introduced and demonstrated using a monolingual practice. In this chapter, the methodology was applied to a first bilingual practice, namely language choice in the interactional site of speech representation. As in the case of the monolingual practice, a phenomenon was noticed as having been frequently reported in the literature and supplementary questions were raised. In the particular case, the question was: how exactly does language choice in the specific site of DSR work? The question arose precisely because there appeared to be diversity in the practice. Therefore in the search for an answer to the question, the first step has been, drawing on a corpus of data, to systematise that diversity. This led to the observation that, among bilingual speakers, DSR may, but need not, adopt the medium of the 'original' event. Thus, the research question was respecified as that of how to account for this diversity. Previous theoretical knowledge of how DSR works in interaction in general – notably, the demonstration theory by Clark and Gerrig (1990) – was adopted as a working hypothesis. A key claim in this theory is that DSR is not a mere reproduction of a previous event, but rather a creation of current participants. In turn, this led to yet another respecification of the issue at hand. The issue became, not why 'original' medium is maintained or not, but rather why current medium is sometimes deviated from. A second claim of the model is that anything that speakers can recognisably demonstrate can be reported. The claim led us to the observation that language choice itself can be reported. We spoke of medium reporting in this case and argued that the first step in understanding how language choice in DSR works is in terms of the contrast +medium reporting versus –medium reporting. In the first case, 'original' medium has to be retained. Clark and Gerrig's model further claims that, in DSR, an element can be depictive, it can be incidental and it can be supportive. This led us to distinguish, in the case of medium reporting, two distinct situations, namely the situation where language choice is incidental and

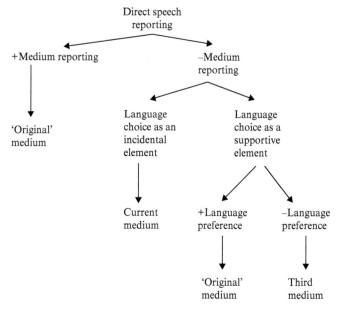

Figure 4.2   Speech representation and bilingualism as an interactional practice

the situation where it is a supportive element. In the first case, current medium is used, whether it corresponds to the medium of the 'original' event or not. In the second, 'original' medium may be used so long as it does not run across participants' language preferences. If it does, compromise strategies, such as using yet a third medium, are adopted. In a nutshell, then, the application of the methodology proposed in Chapter 3 reveals that, at the level of DSR, bilingualism as an interactional practice is organised as in Figure 4.2.

Note

1. Both terms will be used interchangeably.

5 Language choice and conversational repair in bilingual interaction

5.1 Introduction

In addition to speech representation, conversational repair is one of the interactional sites in which CS has frequently been reported to occur (e.g. Gumperz, 1982; Auer, 1984; Wei, 1994; Alfonzetti, 1998; Shin and Milroy, 2000; Gafaranga, 2000; Ihemere, 2007, etc.). Yet, despite these frequent 'noticings', just as in the case of DSR, no systematic account of repair in bilingual conversation has yet been proposed. To be sure, working under a very strong influence of what, in the last chapter, I have referred to as the contextualisation assumption, researchers have commented on CS in repair sequences as mainly, if not only, serving a signalling function through language contrast (Auer, 1988 / 2000: 176). In this respect, Alfonzetti writes:

> Code-switching (. . .) can work as a self-repair technique, as an alternative or together with other techniques normally used in monolingual discourse, like self-interruption, vowel lengthening, hesitation pauses, repetition etc. (Alfonzetti, 1998: 186–7)

That is, according to this view, CS functions as a repair marker. Evidence in support of this view can be found in cases such as Extract 5.1 below, where the choice of English in the repair initiator in turn 2 highlights this function through contrast with the choice of Chinese in the reparandum (Milroy and Wei, 1995: 151).

Extract 5.1 (Milroy and Wei, 1995)

```
1. A:  . . . koei hai yisaang.
          [He's a doctor.]
2. B:  Is he?
3. A:  Yichin (.) hai Hong Kong.
          [Before] [In Hong Kong]
```

However, the same cannot be said of English–French CS in the following instance of conversational repair. Here, what matters is not so much that the choice of French contrasts with that of English, but rather that language choice itself, the choice of English in this case, is the problem to be repaired.

Extract 5.2

```
1. D:  Ufite homework – devoir
2. A:  Ahaaa Ni ikibazo gikomeye

    ---------------------------

1. D:  You have a homework – homework
2. A:  Ahaa It's a big problem
```

Also consider Extract 5.3 below. In the example, it is not the case that the switch from Kinyarwanda to French in turn 2 merely signals repair for, if it were, there would be no need for first speaker to adopt the same French item in turn 3.

Extract 5.3

```
1. A:  (. . .) ariko kenshi biterwa n'ukuntu (.) na
       mwarimu wawe
2. B:  directeur
3. A:  eh ton directeur (.) ton direct- iyo ari umu-
       directeur w'umugome ushobara no kumara imyaka
       itanu (. . .)

    ---------------------------

1. A:  often it depends on (.) on your teacher
2. B:  supervisor
3. A:  yes your supervisor (.) your superv- if your
       supervisor is a cruel person you can even
       spend five years (. . .)
```

Briefly, as regards CS in conversational repair in bilingual interaction, it is clear that the contextualisation assumption is very limited. There is a need for an account of how exactly language choice interacts with repair in bilingual conversation. As an interactional practice, conversational repair has been widely investigated (see, for example, Liddicoat, 2007, and Sidnell, 2010, for reviews) and the body of empirical knowledge which has been generated can be drawn upon in developing an understanding of how language choice works in this interactional practice. Given this knowledge about repair as a conversational practice, two research questions can be asked with respect to language choice: (1) where in the repair sequence can language alternation occur? and (2) what does language alternation do when it occurs in repair sequences? This chapter addresses these two questions by way of another example of how bilingualism can be investigated as an interactional practice.

5.2 Language alternation and the organisation of repair in bilingual conversation

As I have indicated above, conversational repair is one of the features of conversational organisation which have attracted ample research attention. This body of accumulated knowledge shows that, maximally, a repair sequence comprises four components: *repairable* or *trouble source*, *repair initiator*, *repairer* and *ratification*. In investigating the question of where in the repair sequence language alternation may occur, I will consider each of these components.

5.2.1 Language choice as / in repairable

A key finding of the research on conversational repair is that nothing in the talk is, in principle, excludable from the class 'repairable' (Schegloff et al., 1977: 363). Any significant aspect of talk organisation can be a source of difficulty in conversation and, therefore, a repairable. Here is some evidence. In Extract 5.4 below, a lexico-grammatical problem arises. Participants are saying that the natives of the country where they live are racist ('do not like foreigners'). Evidence of this racism is found in the question they typically ask any foreign student: namely, whether he / she is studying in order to go back and work in his / her country of origin. A designs his turn such that an adjective is expected after the verb form 'ari' (are). That is, a subject + verb + complement (SVC) construction is projected. However, a problem arises, as this adjective is not readily available to the speaker. Initially, A retraces himself while searching for the adjective. Failing to find it, he abandons the search and the syntactic construction he had projected, and adopts a subject + verb + object (SVO) construction.

Extract 5.4

```
A:  Ikikwereka ukunta ari ntuza- ari— badakunda aban-
    yamahanga iwabo (.) baraza bakakubaza (.) uri
    kwiga iki ah ngo c'est pour aller travailler dans
    ton pays ((laughter))
```

```
A:  What shows you that they are something- they are-
    they don't like foreigners (.) they come and ask
    you (.) what are you studying is it to go and
    work in your country? ((laughter))
```

In Extract 5.5, on the other hand, a problem of hearing / understanding arises. Participants are talking about a party which E and other girl members of a dance group have attended. To the question of how many girls were involved, she answers that there were twenty-five of them (turn 10). In turn 11, C uses an *open class repair initiator* (Drew, 1997; see also below) and E responds by restating the number 'twenty-five' (12), thus confirming that she has understood C's 'umh?' as indicating lack of hearing.

Extract 5.5

```
1.  C:  Vous étiez combien à peu près? (Estimations)?
(. . .)
10. E:  Euh il y avait vingt-cinq- je crois
11. C:  umh?
12. E:  vingt-cinq
13. C:  C'est beaucoup euh

----------------------------

1.  C:  How many were you roughly? (on average?)
(. . .)
10. E:  Euh there were twenty-five — I think
11. C:  Umh?
12. E:  Twenty-five
13. C:  That's a lot
```

In Extract 5.6, a problem arises at the level of what pragmaticists refer to as the *illocutionary force* (Searle, 1969) of what is said. Talk involves a health visitor (HV), a father (F) and a mother (M). A baby is feeding. The health visitor makes a comment to the effect that the baby is enjoying his food. The health visitor's statement is interpreted differently by the father and the mother. The father seems to have taken it to be a plain statement and agrees with it. The mother, on the other hand, seems to have taken it to have the implication that the baby has not been fed (by her), finds this implication offensive (Heritage and Sefi, 1992: 367) and repairs it by way of challenging it.

Extract 5.6 (Heritage and Sefi, 1992)

```
1. HV:  He's enjoying that [isn't he.
```

```
2. F:   [Yes, he certainly is =
3. M:   =He's not hungry 'cuz (h)he's just had 'iz
        bo:ttle.hhh
```

Also consider Extract 5.7 below. In the conversation, participant A, a Rwandan priest living in Belgium, is saying that his parishioners trust him so much that they often come to tell him their personal problems. In turn 2, B uses a repair strategy (*exposed correction*; Jefferson, 1987) to formulate the *gist* (Heritage and Watson, 1979) of A's talk. Unlike in Extract 5.5, here repair is used to communicate understanding and alignment between the participants.

Extract 5.7

```
1. A:   (. . .) aho kugirango ajye kwa Psy atange igi-
        humbi antumaho rero ni hahandi ni ukuvuga
        akavuga
2. B:   akakubwira
3. A:   akambwira
4. B:   N'ubundi ni cyo abapadiri baberaho hano mu
        burayi
```

```
1. A:   Instead of going to the Psy(chiatrist) and
        paying one thousand (Belgian Francs) they send
        for me it the same it's to talk they talk (to
        me)
2. B:   they tell you
3. A:   they tell me
4. B:   that's exactly the role of priests here in
        Europe
```

As I have argued elsewhere, language choice is a significant aspect of talk organisation (Gafaranga, 1999). Therefore, among bilingual speakers, a repairable may arise at the level of language choice. Extract 5.2 is a case in point. In the example, the choice of English is felt to be a problem and repaired using French. A similar situation arises in Extract 5.8 below, where the choice of Kinyarwanda in turn 1 is felt to be a problem and repaired.

Extract 5.8

1. C: Yuu! **Mwali nka bangahe?** (.) *Vous étiez combien à peu près?* *(Estimations)?*

2. E: *Toutes les filles ou tout le groupe?*

3. C: *Tout le- tout le groupe a dansé?*
4. E: *Pas tout le- tout le groupe*

----

1. C: Yuu! How many were you roughly? (.) *How many were you roughly?*
         (O*n average?*)
2. E: *All the girls or the whole group?*
3. C: *Did the- the whole group dance?*
4. E: *Not the- the whole group*

Of course, in conversation, repairables do not occur pre-tagged, as it
were, as having to do with language choice. In some cases, the recognition of the actual nature of a repairable as having to do with language
choice is an interactional achievement. Here is an example. Talk
involves an adult participant (B) and a child (E).

Extract 5.9

1. B: *Alors E, washushanyije iki?*
2. E: **Quoi?**
3. B: *Ça c´est quoi?*
4. (.)
5. B: *Qu´est ce que tu as dessiné?*

----

1. B: *So E, what have you drawn?*
2. E: **What?**
3. B: *What is this?*
4. (.)
5. B: *What have you drawn?*

In turn 1, B produces a *first pair part* (Schegloff and Sacks, 1973) using
Kinyarwanda. In turn 2, E uses an *open-class repair initiator* (Drew, 1997)
and, at the same time, switches from Kinyarwanda to French. In 3, B
attends to both the content and the language choice dimensions of the
repair initiator. At the level of content, B produces a modified version
of his initial question, moving from 'washushanyije iki?' (what have you
drawn?) to '*ça c'est quoi?*' (what is this?), as if E's difficulty has been that
of understanding. At the level of language choice, he switches from his
prior use of Kinyarwanda to French. Interestingly, when no second pair
part is produced after this ambivalent repair (pause in 4), B re-analyses
the repairable as having only a language choice dimension and translates his original first pair part into French.

5.2.2   Language alternation and / in repair initiation

The second component of a repair sequence is the repair initiator. At this level, a distinction is made between *self-initiation* and *other-initiation*. In turn, in self-initiation of repair, speakers use a variety of non-lexical speech perturbations such as cutoffs and voicings like 'er' and 'hm' (Schegloff et al., 1977: 367). As these non-verbal devices are not language-specific, they can be found both in monolingual and in bilingual conversation. Therefore, they are inconsequential for the relationship between language alternation and conversational repair. A more interesting observation regarding self-initiation of repair is that it need not result in self-repair. Current speaker may notice / anticipate a problem but fail to find the repairer. In this case, other-repair may be produced (Schegloff et al., 1977: 364). Consider Extract 5.10 below.

Extract 5.10

```
1. A:  n'ibintu by mu Rutonde bavugango bakore ikinyar-
       wandaaa (.) kitagize-
2. B:      [pure
3. C:      [pure
4. A:  umh ibyo narabirwayaga dès le début

-----------------------------

1. A:  like the commission of Rutonde who were develop-
       ing Kinyarwandaaa (.) which was-
2. B:      [pure
3. C:      [pure
4. A:  I was against that from the very beginning
```

A initiates repair, but the repairer is produced by B and C in overlapping turns.

Given the fact that any aspect of talk organisation is potentially repairable, this possibility of other-repair after self-initiation raises a practical problem. How does next speaker know exactly which aspect of the talk first speaker wanted to repair? This is the exact opposite of a problem Sidnell (2010) refers to as the *other-initiated repair problem*. Paraphrasing this, we can speak of a *self-initiated other-repair problem*. A recurrent strategy speakers use to overcome this practical difficulty is for current speaker to give clues as to what the repairable is. In Extract 5.10, for example, the item 'kitagize' ('which was') clues interlocutors to the fact that current speaker is trying to qualify the kind of Kinyarwanda which was being promoted. Among bilingual speakers, language alternation can be used as a resource in attending to this practical problem of cluing interlocutors to the repairable. Consider Extract 5.11 below.

> Extract 5.11 (Torras, 1999, cited in Gafaranga, 2005)
>
> ```
> 1. STU:  I'm sorry it's not your fault right
> 2. SEC:  no [uh no that's you- you- you-
> 3. STU:  [I'm erm I offended you
> 4. SEC:  mmm (.) LE LE DROIT LE (to RES) el dret
> 5. RES:  the right
> 6. SEC:  the right (.) you have the right to protest
>          eh OK
> ```
>
> ----------------------------
>
> ```
> 4. SEC:  mmm (.) the the right the (to RES) the right
> ```

Talk takes place in an Erasmus office on a university campus in Barcelona. The participants involved are a Catalan-origin secretary (SEC), a student from Germany (STU) and a Catalan-origin researcher (RES). In terms of *language preferences* (Auer, 1984; Gafaranga, 2001; Torras and Gafaranga, 2002), all three participants can speak English, SEC and RES share Catalan (and Spanish), and SEC can also speak French. In the conversation, English has been adopted as the medium. In turns 2 and 4, SEC has a problem finding the word for what she wants to say and uses different strategies to initiate repair, namely repetition and cutoffs 'you- you- you', the word search marker 'mmm' and the pause (.) (Schegloff et al., 1977: 367). Failing to find the solution to her problem, she invites the support of co-participants in order to overcome the difficulty. But, as co-participants cannot read her mind (cannot tell which word she is missing), a practical problem arises of how to make it clear to them exactly what it is that she is having problems with. To solve this problem, she switches first to French (upper case) and then to Catalan (underlined).

A second instance of this use of CS as a resource for solving the self-initiated other-repair problem can be found in Extract 5.12. Participants have adopted Kinyarwanda–French language alternation as the medium. In the course of his talk, A comes across a problem of the *mot juste* for what he wants to say. After many unsuccessful attempts, he seeks his co-participant's support and uses German (Sozialamt) by way of indicating exactly what it is that he is having problems with. In turn 2, B attempts other-repair, which, unfortunately, is not accepted as appropriate (turn 3).

Extract 5.12

```
1. A:  kwenregistra umwan a n'ibiki (.) byose kugi-
       rango donc (.) abone amafaranga- donc kugi-
       ranga (unclear) (.) bon ((laughter)) njya muri
       ntuza- muri za ministères- murii (.) Sozialamt
       (.) donc ni kimwe-
2. B:  ministère des affaires sociales
3. A:  oya (.) ni service en fait ntabwo ari ministère
```

```
1. A:  registering the child and so on (.) all that
       so (.) she receives the money (.) well so
       that (unclear) so I went to something- to the
       ministry departments (.) to the (.) social
       welfare office (.) well it's like-
2. B:  Ministry of Social Affairs
3. A:  no (.) in fact it's an office it's not a ministry
```

We have seen above that, at the level of repair initiation, a distinction must be made between self-initiation and other-initiation. In turn, other-initiation takes many forms, including *open class repair initiators*, *class-specific question words*, *repetition with or without question words* and *understanding checks* (Schegloff et al., 1977: 367–9). Among bilingual speakers, language alternation may co-occur with each of these. To start with the first form, Drew (1997: 71) defines an open class repair initiator as one which does not locate specifically what it is in the prior turn that the speaker is having trouble with hearing or understanding. An open class repair initiator does not locate a specific repairable in the prior turn. When an open repair initiator is used, a speaker indicates that he / she has some difficulty with the other's prior turn, but without locating specifically where or what that difficulty is. Usually, open class repair initiators are interpreted as indicating a general problem of understanding / hearing. Extract 5.9 above is a good case in point. As we have seen, B is unsure about exactly what the problem, as perceived by E, is. This is precisely because E's repair initiator 'quoi' is not specific as to its object. Incidentally, the same example shows that open class repair initiators may involve language alternation. Also consider Extract 5.13.

Extract 5.13

```
1. B:  Uzaza kunsura ryari?
2. C:  Quoi?
```

```
3. B:  Uzaza kunsura ryari?
4. C:  Je ne sais pas
5. B:  Urabizi sha
```

```
1. B:  When are you coming to visit me?
2. C:  What?
3. B:  When are you coming to visit me?
4. C:  I don't know
5. B:  You do know, come on
```

In this example, B has interpreted the repair initiator as indicating only a lack of hearing / understanding. Indeed, following the initiator, he restates his first pair part in the same language. However, given the fact that, in turn 4, C does not converge towards B's choice of Kinyarwanda strongly suggests that C's problem is actually that of language choice. That is, the unspecified nature of the repair initiator has led to a misunderstanding between the participants. Either way, what is noteworthy for us here and now is that the repair initiator involves language alternation.

Unlike open class repair initiators, class-specific question words point to specific items in prior talk as the repairables. An instance of this can be found in Extract 5.1, where the repair initiator 'is he?' points back to 'doctor' in turn 1. Here again, the repair initiator involves CS from Chinese to English. An example from the Rwandan context can be found in Extract 5.14. In the sequence, a mother (A) instructs her daughter (C) to count so as to display her fluency in Kinyarwanda. However, the mother does not specify in which language the child should count. As a result, C initiates repair using a specific question designed to elicit the name of a specific language. At the same time, she switches from Kinyarwanda (as used by the mother in turn 1) to French. In turn 3, the mother effects repair, indicating the specific language (Kinyarwanda).

Extract 5.14

```
1. A:  C, ngaho nawe bara turebe
2. C:  En quoi?
3. A:  En kinyarwanda
4. C:  (unclear)
```

```
1. A:  C, show us how you can count
2. C:  In which (language)?
```

3. A: *In Kinyarwanda*
4. C: (unclear)

The third strategy for other-initiated repair is repetition with or without a question word. An example of this strategy can be found in Extract 5.15 below. Talk takes place in a Rwandan family in Belgium. Visitor B is amazed at child C's sport skills (talk not shown) and asks her who taught her to do sports. In turn 2, C provides a second pair part. In turn 3, B initiates repair, using repetition, by way of opening a *non-minimal post-expansion sequence* (Schegloff, 2007).

Extract 5.15

1. B: Ni nde wakwigishije?
2. C: *Moi toute seule*
3. B: ***Toute seule?***
4. C: *Les copines qui m´ont montrée*

----

1. B: Who taught you to do it?
2. C: (I learned) *all by myself*
3. B: (you learned) **all by yourself?**
4. C: *Some friends showed me (how to do it)*

Among bilingual speakers, repetition may involve language alternation, as in Extracts 5.16 and 5.17 below.

Extract 5.16

1. B: E, mubyinire gato arebe (.) bimwe bya *un deux trois* chu chu chu– bya bindi byaa– **mwakoze kugeza kuri** *onze*
2. E: ***Que j´ai fait jusqu´à onze?***
3. B: Ubare kugeza kuri *onze* (.) ya nkoni yawe iri hariya genda uyizane kugirango ubare kugeza kuri *onze*
----
1. B: Dance a bit for him to see (.) the one you go *one two three* chu chu chu– the one you– **you did up to eleven**
2. E: ***The one I did up to eleven?***
3. B: You count up to *eleven* (.) Your stick is there go and get it so you can count up to *eleven*

Extract 5.17

```
1. E:  Je lui ai posé toutes les questions que j'avais
2. A:  Byose?
3. E:  Oui
-----------------------------
1. E:  I have asked him all the questions I had
2. A:  All of them?
3. E:  Yes
```

Note that, in this strategy as in all the others, language choice itself may, but need not, be oriented to as the repairable. In the examples above, language choice is not oriented to as repairable as evidenced by the fact that, in turn 3, first speaker maintains his / her language choice as in turn 1. In Extract 5.18 below, on the other hand, language choice itself is the repairable, as evinced by the fact that, in turn 3, the only action A undertakes following C's repair initiation is to switch from Kinyarwanda to French.

Extract 5.18

```
1. A:  Uzi kubara?
2. C:  Je sais compter?
3. A:  Tu sais compter?
4. C:  Oui
5. E:  Jusqu'à combien?
-----------------------------
1. A:  Do you know how to count?
2. C:  Do I know how to count?
3. A:  Do you know how to count?
4. C:  Yes
5. E:  Up to how much?
```

The last strategy for other-initiation of repair is to propose a possible understanding of prior turn (Schegloff et al., 1977: 368). Among bilinguals, possible understanding of prior turn can be revealed through CS. Consider Extract 5.19. Talk takes place in a bilingual Rwandan family in Belgium. B, the visitor, asks C, a child, how many friends he has. As B, in 2, produces what appears to be an irrelevant second pair part, A, the mother, steps in to clarify the first pair part. C encounters a problem in following A's talk and calls for repair, suggesting a candidate solution. The actual problem has to do with the word 'umubare' (number). Using French, C puts forth what he considers this term to mean (*sœur*) and calls for A's confirmation. In so doing, he switches from Kinyarwanda to French. Unfortunately, as revealed in turn 5, A does not confirm C's proposed understanding.

Extract 5.19

1. B: Ufite inshuti zingahe?
2. C: *Au Rwanda j'ai aussi des amis*
3. A: Yakubajije hano- mu Rwanda ntaho yakubajije-
       mu Rwanda ntabo uzi. Atangiye kwibagirwa
       kubera *vacances*. Yakubajije **umubare w'inshuti
       zawe**
4. C: **La sœur?**
5. A: Umubare

----

1. B: How many friends do you have?
2. C: *I have friends in Rwanda too*
3. A: He asked you about here- he didn't ask you about
       Rwanda- You do not know anybody in Rwanda. He is
       starting to forget because of the *holidays*. He
       asked you the number of your friends
4. C: **The sister?**
5. A: The number

5.2.3 Language alternation and / in the repairer

The third element in a repair sequence is the repairer. With respect to
this element, two related questions are asked. Who produces it – that
is, who effects repair – and where does the repairer appear relative
to the trouble source? With respect to the first of the two questions,
a distinction must be made between *self-repair* and *other-repair*. In
terms of position relative to the trouble source, three different positions are possible for self-repair and one for other-repair, except if
repair has been delayed (Schegloff, 2000). For self-repair, the possible
positions are: within the same turn constructional unit (TCU) as the
trouble source (*same turn repair*), in the next TCU after the one containing the trouble source (*transition space repair*) and in the third turn
after the one containing the trouble source (*third position repair*). An
example of same turn repair involving no language alternation can
be found in Extract 5.4 above, reproduced below as Extract 5.20 for
convenience.

Extract 5.20

A: Ikikwereka ukunta **ari   ntuza-   ari—   badakunda**
    abanyamahanga iwabo (.) baraza bakakubaza (.) uri

```
      kwiga iki ah ngo c'est pour aller travailler dans
      ton pays ((laughter))

      ---------------------------

A:    What shows you that they are something- they are-
      they don't like foreigners (.) they come and ask
      you (.) what are you studying is it to go and
      work in your country? ((laughter))
```

As we have seen, in the extract, A had projected an SVC construction with the verb 'ari' (is). Missing the adjective to complete the SVC structure and therefore the TCU, he aborts the projected construction and resumes the TCU with an SVO construction. Among bilingual speakers, same turn repair involving language alternation is very common. Here is an example. In this piece of talk, a word search problem arises (see elongation in 'wakoraaa') and the speaker solves it by switching from Kinyarwanda to French, thus completing the TCU in two languages.

Extract 5.21

```
C:    Naho iNairobi se wakoraaa — sur quelle base?

      ---------------------------

C:    As for Nairobi how can you work?'
```

As for transition space repair, two possibilities can be found. In the first case, a complete TCU is produced and then replaced by another one, as in Extract 5.22 below, where 'What do you take?' is replaced by 'Do you try anything?'.

Extract 5.22 (Gafaranga and Britten, 2004)

```
D:    What do you take? Do you try anything?
P:    Well I try that (Agro- Agroca- and er Agrocar) is
      that you gave me
D:    Right.
```

Alternatively, a complete TCU is produced and then an element within it is repaired. In Extract 5.23, a complete TCU ('more people will show up. Cuz they won't feel obligated to sell') is produced and then an element within it ('to sell') is repaired, replacing it by another ('to buy').

Extract 5.23 (Schegloff et al., 1977, cited in Liddicoat, 2007)

```
B:    -then more people will show up. Cuz they won't
      feel obligated to sell. Tuh buy.
```

Among bilingual speakers, language alternation can be involved in both types of transition space repair. For instance, Extract 5.2 is a case where an element within a first TCU is repaired in another TCU, using a different language. In Extract 5.8, on the other hand, a whole TCU is replaced by a new one in a different language. Another instance of the second possibility is Extract 5.24 below. In turn 1, B asks C how he feels when he speaks Kinyarwanda, first in Kinyarwanda and then in French.

Extract 5.24

```
1. B:  Ikinyarwanda iyo ukivugaa (.) wumva- wumva
       bimeze gute? Comment te sens-tu quand tu
       parles le kinyarwanda?
2. C:  Moi je ne parle pas souvent
```

```
1. B:  When you speak Kinyarwanda (.) how do
       you feel? How do you feel when you speak
       Kinyarwanda?
2. C:  I do not speak it that often
```

Finally, instances of third position repair can be found in the many examples involving other-repair initiation we have looked at above. The repair initiation occupies the second position, leading first speaker to self-repair in position 3. Also note that, as in Extracts 5.13, 5.16 and 5.17, language alternation may occur between the repair initiator and the repairer.

As I have said above, a distinction is made between self-repair and other-repair. While three positions are available for self-repair (see above), one is normatively available for other-repair, namely second position (except if repair has been delayed and occurs in the fourth position) (Schegloff, 2000). In the following, I consider only second position repair, the standard format. In second position repair, a distinction is made between *self-initiated other-repair* and *other-initiated other-repair*. Many of the examples we have examined consist of self-initiated other-repair (e.g. Extracts 5.11 and 5.12) and they involve language alternation (e.g. Extract 5.10).

As for other-initiated other-repair, a distinction is made between *exposed correction* and *embedded correction* (Jefferson, 1987). A main feature of exposed correction is that, uninvited, it interrupts the flow of the on-going activity. Cases of exposed correction involving language alternation can be found in Extract 5.25 and Extract 5.26. (Extract 3 above reproduced here for convenience.)

Extract 5.25

```
1. A:  ni mukuru (.) agako- agatourna uko ashaka
2. B:  à son rythme
3. A:  à son rythme
4. B:  ((laughter))
```

```
1. A:  He's mature (.) runs it (printer) as he wants
2. B:  at his own pace
3. A:  at his own pace
4. B:  ((laughter))
```

Extract 5.26

```
1. A:  ariko kenshi biterwa n'ukuntu (.) na mwarimu
       wawe
2. B:  directeur
3. A:  eh ton directeur (.) ton direct- iyo ari umu-
       directeur w'umugome ushobara no kumara imyaka
       itanu
```

```
1. A:  often it depends on (.) on your teacher
2. B:  supervisor
3. A:  yes your supervisor (.) your superv- if your
       supervisor is a cruel person you can even spend five
       years
```

Embedded correction contrasts sharply with exposed correction in the sense that the repairer is integrated in the on-going activity. Consider Extract 5.27 below. Talk takes place in a Rwandan family in Belgium. Participants have been talking about C's birthday and he says that he had a nice birthday cake. B assumes that the cake was home-made and wants to know who made it in a first pair part. B produces a second pair part which attends to the point of the question (*on* – we) and at the same time repairs the assumption that the cake was homemade by saying that it was actually bought. In addition to doing all this, he switches from Kinyarwanda to French.

Extract 5.27

```
1. B:  Ni nde wayiteguye?
2. C:  On l'a acheté
```

```
3. B:  Mama yaguhaye cadeau?
4. C:  Non
```

```
1. B:  Who prepared it?
2. C:  We bought it
3. B:  Did your mum give you a present?
4. C:  No
```

This notion of embedded correction is particularly important at the level of language choice. As we have seen, language choice itself may be the repairable. As a consequence, speakers may choose to repair it in an embedded fashion, as in Extract 5.28 below (Extract 5.15 expanded). In turn 1, B asks C whether he knows how to do sports using Kinyarwanda. In turn 2, C provides a relevant second pair part, but using French. In turn 6, B asks C who taught her how to do sports, once again using Kinyarwanda. In turn 7, C provides a relevant second pair part, but once again in French. In 8, B initiates a post-expansion and, interestingly, he too uses French. That is, the choice of Kinyarwanda by B is repaired in a way that does not disrupt the flow of talk. It is for this reason that, elsewhere (Gafaranga, 2010), I have used the term *embedded medium repair* to describe cases like this.

Extract 5.28

```
1. B:  Uzi gukora sports burya?'
2. C:  Oui
(. . .)
6. B:  Ni nde wakwigishije?
7. C:  Moi toute seule
8. B:  Toute seule?
9. C:  Les copines qui m´ont montrée
```

```
1. B:  So you know how to do sports?
2. C:  Yes
(. . .)
6. B:  Who taught you to do it?
7. C:  (I learned) all by myself
8. B:  (you learned) all by yourself?
9. C:  Some friends showed me (how to do it)
```

This possibility of embedded correction at the level of language choice forces a re-analysis of language alternation in other-initiation

```
Turn 1: X
Turn 2: Y
Turn 3: Y
```

Figure 5.1   The structure of embedded correction

```
Turn 1: X
Turn 2: Y
Turn 3: X/Y
```

Figure 5.2   Language choice in embedded correction

of repair. According to Jefferson (1987), correction, either exposed or embedded, has the structure shown in Figure 5.1. Obviously, if repair has not been successful, turn 3 may take the form X. This same structure can be applied to language choice in each of the examples where language alternation has been observed in other-initiation of repair. More specifically, each of the examples fits the pattern shown in Figure 5.2, where X and Y stand for languages. That is to say, instead of viewing language alternation as merely co-occurring with other levels of repair organisation, it must be viewed as forming a repair sequence in its own right, a sequence in which language choice in position 2 functions as a repairer. In turn, this repair process must be seen as an embedded one in the sense that language alternation does not interrupt the on-going activity. That is to say, repair at the level of language choice is accomplished in addition to whatever else participants are doing. More specifically, it is accomplished in addition to whatever other repair action is going on (be it initiation of repair by means of an open repair initiator, by means of specific class question word, by means of repetition, etc.). In turn, this re-analysis is in line with Auer's view (1998) that language choice can be seen as an autonomous level of conversational organisation and that speakers orient to it simultaneously as whatever else they are doing.

5.2.4   Language alternation and / in repair ratification

In the structure for correction as proposed by Jefferson (1987) (see above), ratification corresponds to the third position. Extracts where the structure applies perfectly well are Extracts 5.7, 5.25 and 5.26. Can language alternation occur in the ratification slot? The structure as proposed by Jefferson and indeed the data we have examined suggest that, if repair has been successful, language alternation in the ratification slot is impossible. This would appear to be the case, particularly if ratification consists of repetition. In the case where repair has not been successful, would language alternation be possible? Lacking appropriate data, I am not in a position to provide a general answer to this question. However, in the specific situation when language choice itself is the repairable, there is plenty of evidence that, when repair has failed, language alternation occurs in the ratification slot. As we have seen above, repair at the level of language choice is often done in an embedded fashion. When repair is successful, first speaker abandons his / her original choice and accommodates to next speaker's choice, thus realising a perfect X–Y–Y structure (see above for examples of this). However, when the proposed repairer (Y) in position 2 is rejected, first speaker maintains his / her original choice (X), and this realises the structure X–Y–X. In this case, language alternation occurs at the level of the ratification slot. Situations where the X–Y–X structure is observed, i.e. situations in which language alternation occurs at the level of the ratification slot, include examples such as 5.16, 5.17 and 5.27.

To summarise, close observation of the data shows that, in bilingual conversation, language alternation and conversational repair are intimately intertwined. Language alternation can occur at any point in the repair sequence. The fact that language alternation can occur anywhere in the repair sequence strongly suggests that its function cannot be reduced to signalling repair, i.e. it points to the limitation of the contextualisation assumption. Indeed, if, in line with Gumperz (1982), we take the role of contextualisation cues to be to set inferential processes in motion, it seems counter-intuitive that the inferential process would be triggered, as in the case of language alternation in the ratification slot, at the completion of the sequence which needs to be interpreted. At best, the contextualisation assumption can be supported only if, as in the case of Milroy and Wei (1995), observation is limited to language choice at the level of repair initiation. Thus, the issue of the role of language choice in conversational repair in bilingual interaction has to be looked at again in light of the understanding of the repair sequence as we have developed it so far. It is to this issue that I now turn.

5.3   The functionality of language choice in repair sequences

In approaching the issue of the functionality of language alternation in conversational repair, it is important to recall Auer's observation that, in bilingual conversation participants have two types of tasks. First, there are problems specifically addressed to language choice (...). Secondly, participants have to solve a number of problems (...) related to the organisation of conversation in general. The alternate use of two languages may be a means of coping with these (two sets of) problems. (Auer, 1988 / 2000: 170)

This distinction between the two levels is further highlighted, as we have seen, by Gafaranga (1999), where I explicitly state that language choice itself is a significant aspect of talk organisation. Also, we recall that, according to Schegloff, any significant aspect of talk organisation can be the focus of repair (Schegloff et al., 1977: 363). Extrapolating, we can safely say that language choice itself can be the focus of repair. Indeed, throughout the last section, I have constantly been pointing this out whenever it was relevant. I therefore propose that, in thinking about the functionality of language choice in repair sequences, the first question to ask is: is this instance of repair focused on language choice per se or not? Alternatively, we may ask: does language choice in this instance of repair contribute to the organisation of repair at levels other than language choice? In other words, we could ask: is language choice in this instance to be seen as an additional resource for the organisation of repair? A convenient way of referring to this basic distinction is to use the term '*medium repair*' when referring to the first phenomenon and the term '*other-language repair*' when referring to the second phenomenon. Once these initial questions are answered, we can then ask specific ones about the exact level of repair organisation to which language choice contributes. Answers to these two sets of questions will lead to the following possibilities and therefore to

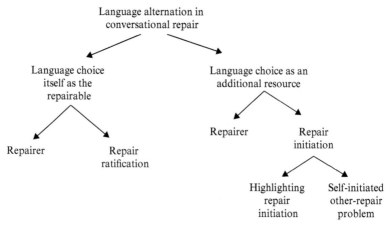

Figure 5.3   Language choice in conversational repair

the diagram shown in Figure 5.3, which, I would like to propose, depicts language choice in conversational repair as an interactional practice.

The figure reads as follows:

1. LANGUAGE CHOICE ITSELF MAY BE THE REPAIRABLE.
2. If (1), a repairer, involving language alternation, may follow in the form of either (a) self-repair or (b) other-medium repair.
   or
3. If 2, language alternation may occur in the repair ratification slot by way of rejecting the proposed medium (repairer).
4. LANGUAGE CHOICE MAY BE AN ADDITIONAL RESOURCE FOR THE ORGANISATION OF REPAIR.
5. If (4), language alternation may occur in the repairer in the form of self-repair or other-language repair.
   or
6. If (4), language alternation may occur in the initiation of repair.
7. If (6), language alternation may occur to highlight the initiation of repair.
   or
8. If (6), language alternation may occur to solve the self-initiated other-repair problem.

5.4   Summary and conclusion

Researchers have consistently reported sightings of language alternation in conversational repair in bilingual conversation. However, language choice in conversational repair has not been focused on as such. This chapter has sought to go beyond these 'noticings' and propose an account of the practice, specifically addressing the relationship between language alternation and conversational repair. Two specific questions were raised: (1) where in repair organisation can language alternation occur? and (2) what does language alternation do when it occurs in repair sequences? In order to address these issues, the body of knowledge already existing on conversational repair in general was applied to bilingual data and a specific understanding of the practice emerged. In bilingual conversation, language choice interacts with repair organisation in two ways. Either language choice itself is the focus of repair or it is an additional resource for the organisation of repair. In both cases, the understanding developed adds back to the existing body of knowledge on conversational repair. In the first case, this analysis confirms Schegloff's view that nothing in the talk is, in principle, excludable from the class 'repairable' (Schegloff et al., 1977: 363) and, conversely, that language choice itself is a significant aspect of talk organisation (Gafaranga, 1999). In the second case, this finding adds to the existing knowledge about what Sidnell (2010) terms the technology of repair. Sidnell speaks of this technology in relation to self-repair and defines it as consisting of practices for marking the onset and completion of repair, for locating repairable items and for performing some operation upon them (2010: 114). But the need for marking – that is, for signalling – repair is not limited to self-repair; it may also be observed in the case of other-repair. As we have seen, among bilingual speakers, language choice may be used as a resource for highlighting repair initiators and it may be drawn upon in solving the self-initiated other-repair problem. Thus, because this investigation of language choice in conversational repair in bilingual conversation contributes to knowledge about conversational repair in general, it can be described as mainstreamed, mainstreaming being one of the ways in which the study of language alternation in bilingual conversation can continue to be relevant and interesting.

6 Language choice and appositive structures in written texts in Rwanda

6.1 Introduction

The third interactional practice I want to use by way of illustrating how the study of bilingualism, and of language alternation in particular, can be taken forward and continue to be relevant and interesting, now that its initial purpose of rehabilitating bilingualism has largely been achieved, can be termed *translinguistic apposition*. A common definition of apposition (see, for example, Quirk et al., 1985: 1300–20) is as a syntactic structure whereby two noun phrases with a similar meaning are placed next to each other, the second functioning as an explanation, clarification, renaming and so on of the first. In turn, two types of appositive can be found, namely restrictive and non-restrictive appositives. A restrictive appositive significantly narrows the scope of the noun it is appositioned to, while a non-restrictive appositive does not. As a result, a non-restrictive appositive can be deleted without any (major) effect on content, while a restrictive appositive cannot. Consequently, a non-restrictive appositive is set off from the main structure of the sentence, usually by devices such as commas, brackets, dashes and so on, while a restrictive appositive is not. So the difference between the sentence 'Joseph Gafaranga, a Rwandan linguist, currently works at the University of Edinburgh' and the sentence 'The Rwandan linguist Joseph Gafaranga works at the University of Edinburgh' can be explained in terms of the distinction restrictive versus non-restrictive apposition.

In Rwanda, especially in texts Sebba (2002, 2013) describes as 'most highly regulated' (MHR), non-restrictive appositives can be realised bilingually; hence the term *translinguistic apposition*. Here are some examples:

Extract 6.1 (Imyanzuro_y_Umwiherero_w_abayobozi_abakuru_b_ igihugu.pdf.274kB- primature.gov.rw; accessed 12 June 2014)[1]

Gushyiraho politike n'amategeko yo kubaka *amazu aciriritse* (**low cost housing**) no gushyiraho uburyo bunoze bwo kubaka ayo mazu kandi akabonekera ku gihe cyateganyijwe.

To develop policies and regulations on building low cost houses (low cost housing) and appropriate modalities for building those houses such that they are available on time.

Extract 6.1 reproduces the text of one of the recommendations of the most recent Umwiherero w'Igihugu,[2] as posted on the webpage of the Prime Minister's Office (at the time of writing). In the extract, a Kinyarwanda noun phrase (*amazu aciriritse*) is used and, as if to clarify and specify it, an English equivalent (*low cost housing*) is juxtaposed to it. Extract 6.2 comes from the booklet of the manifesto of Itorero ry'Igihugu, a governmental organisation in charge of promoting the Rwandan culture. In the example, the English word *volunteers* is juxtaposed to its Kinyarwanda equivalent as if to clarify its meaning.

Extract 6.2 (*Itorero ry'Igihugu*, p. 23)

ku buryo bw'umwihariko bagira nk'*abakorerabushake* (**volunteers**) mu buryo bwo kwimenyereza imirimo

----

. . . in particular they could have volunteers (volunteers) by way of training for jobs

As for Extract 6.3, it comes from an electronic notice board at the headquarters of the Rwandan Immigration Authority and juxtaposes the Kinyarwanda phrase for 'licence' and its French equivalent.

Extract 6.3 (https://www.migration.gov.rw/Usaba-indi-Passport-mugihe.html; accessed 7 May 2013)

Umucuruzi ugaragaza ko afite ibicuruzwa byangirikira mu mahanga (. . .), akagaragaza n'*icyemezo cy'ubucuruzi* (**registre de commerce**).

A business man / woman who is able to demonstrate that his / her goods are being damaged abroad (. . .) and shows his licence (his licence).

This translanguaging practice may at first be seen as impossible (in the ethnomethodological sense) on theoretical as well as on sociolinguistic grounds. At the theoretical level, the texts in which the practice has been observed, such as those mentioned above, belong to the category Sebba (2002, 2013) describes as 'most highly regulated'. These are (written) texts which are addressed to a wide and anonymous audience. According to Sebba, such texts strongly adhere to the 'ideology of the standard', which, at the level of language choice, translates into a 'monolingual ideology'. Therefore, in such texts, translanguaging is impossible in principle. In addition, in the case of Rwanda, this type of language alternation is in principle impossible, given the country's sociolinguistic context. Rwanda recognises Kinyarwanda, French and English as its official languages, but Rwandans' plurilingual competences form a continuum ranging from monolingualism in Kinyarwanda to trilingualism in Kinyarwanda, French and English, via degrees of Kinyarwanda–French and Kinyarwanda–English bilingualisms. That is, the reality on the ground is that of great diversity in plurilingual competences. In such a context, translanguaging in MHR texts is impossible in principle, as there appears to be a clash between the need for the standard (uniformity) as required by the text-type and the actual diversity on the ground. More concretely, given this diversity and in the absence of any possibility of face-to-face negotiation, there is no guarantee that meanings will be understood as meant and that functions such as explanation and clarification will be served as intended. Therefore, an empirical question, which this chapter will seek to address, is how, in the absence of any predefined standard competence, the observed practice of CS in appositive structures can be accounted for. In the sections which follow, I argue that this possibility of translanguaging in MHR texts in Rwanda can be accounted for by reference to the country's macro language policy. I will demonstrate that the macro language policy allows for trilingualism in Kinyarwanda, French and English to be assumed as standard and, therefore, for translanguaging in MHR texts to be possible. In other words, I will show that the macro policy shapes the local practice and, conversely, that through the very same local practice, the macro language policy is written into being.

6.2 Translinguistic apposition: diverse patterns

Although the practice of CS in appositive structures is routine in MHR texts in Rwanda, in this chapter, a case study methodology will be adopted for in-depth understanding. The practice will be examined with reference to one online news media outlet, namely www.igihe.

com (hereafter Igihe). Igihe is an online media outlet, more precisely a multi-author blog, owned by Igihe Ltd, a media and information technology company registered in Rwanda with the declared purpose of facilitating 'our audience to access fast and reliable news through the internet' (http://en.igihe.com/about-us/; accessed 18 May 2016). The paper[3] is published in three versions, corresponding to the three official languages of Rwanda.[4] Updates, contributed either by Igihe's own staff or by members of the general public, are posted throughout the day. In terms of readership, the intended audience is presumably anybody with internet access, whether Rwandan or not. However, in practice, the actual readership appears to be made up of Rwandans (in Rwanda and in the diaspora). Indeed, even though the paper is available in three language versions, among readers there is a clear preference for Kinyarwanda. To give just one example, a story on Rwandan military personnel (at the time of writing) on a United Nations mission in the Central African Republic was posted in all three languages. The English version came first on 16 February 2014 at 9:22, the Kinyarwanda version was posted a day later on 17 February 2014 at 08:03, and the French version was posted on 17 February 2014 at 09:05. At 12 o'clock on 19 February 2014, the Kinyarwanda page had registered 12,268 hits, 1,854 people had visited the English page, and 1,275 visitors had been registered by the French page. Further evidence of the fact that a Rwandan audience is targeted is the following: an important aspect of Igihe, as any other blog, is the provision for readers' comments. On Igihe, comments are exchanged almost exclusively in Kinyarwanda, even when a story has also been published in the other languages. In terms of the consumption of Igihe texts, the typical literacy event can safely be assumed to be private.[5] The most popular stories on Igihe are those with political content. They register most hits and generate a lot of comments, often expressing anti-government views which, in the current sociopolitical context, could land the author in a great deal of difficulty if identified. Clearly, for such opinions to be expressed, anonymity and therefore privacy have to be assumed. In turn, because of this private nature of the literacy event, in-text practices, including language choice, can be assumed to be standard, i.e. accessible to everybody independently of their linguistic background. Although two types of text can be found on Igihe, namely news articles and readers' comments, for convenience the following discussion will be based almost exclusively on news texts.

Sustained monitoring of Igihe (spanning two years, starting in 2012) generated countless instances of translinguistic apposition. The following are two examples from Igihe:

Extract 6.4 (Isura nshya mu rubanza rwa Mugesera, Igihe, 18 April 2014)

Uburyo bwo gufata amajwi bwasabwe na Mugesera nyuma yo kuvuga ko abanditsi hari byinshi bibacika akifuza ko haba *uwandika inyandiko mu mpine* (**steno dactylog-rapher**), ataboneka hakaba gufata amajwi mu rukiko kw' ibihavugirwa byose.

Mugesera asked for audio recording after he said that transcribers miss a lot of what is said in court. He expressed the wish to see a stenographer (steno dac-tylographer) employed and, failing this, everything which is said in the court audio-recorded.

Extract 6.5 (Kutabonekera igihe kw'imifuka ipakirwamo Sima bidindiza imikorere ya CIMERWA, Igihe, 20 August 2012)

Ku byerekeye igabanya ry'abakozi bagera ku 136 riherutse gukorwa muri CIMERWA, Sekimonyo yavuze ko byaturutse ku nyigo icukumbuye yakozwe n'inzobere mu *micungire y'inganda* (**Industrial Management**) zo muri sosiyete Crowe Howard ikorera mu gihugu cya Kenya, ubwo zerekanaga ko CIMERWA ikeneye abakozi batarenze 125 kugira ngo igabanye *ibitubya umu-tungo* (**Dépenses**) bityo hagakoreshwa abakozi bake bashobora kurushaho gufatwa neza ndetse bakanongera umusaruro.

Regarding the recent retrenchment of almost 136 employ-ees in CIMERWA, Sekimonyo said that it was recommended by a recent report by experts in industrial management (industrial management) from Crowe Howard, a company based in Kenya. The experts said that, in order to reduce its outgoings (expenses), CIMERWA needed no more than 125 employees, who will be very well paid and therefore more productive.

Close examination of the data revealed the following patterns / properties. First of all, as Examples 6.4 and 6.5 show, translan-guaging in appositive structures can take the direction Kinyarwanda–French, just as it can take the direction Kinyarwanda–English. However, although less common, the direction French / English–Kinyarwanda, as in Extracts 6.6 and 6.7, is also possible:

> Extract 6.6 (Dance Group Needs Public Attention, Igihe, 30 November 2011)
>
> ```
> He argued that Rwandans have not been supportive since
> majority prefer hiring traditional dancers (Itorero).
> ```
>
> Extract 6.7 (The Culture Lab Umurage, L'Héritage culturel de Kigali, Igihe, 4 January 2011)
>
> ```
> En plus de ces activités, il s'y passe aussi des veil-
> lées culturelles pendant lesquelles sont donnés des
> concerts de harpes traditionnelles <<Inanga>>, jouées
> par des virtuoses de la harpe.
>
> ----------------------------
>
> In addition to these activities, they also organise
> cultural evenings during which songs are performed
> using traditional harps <<harps>> by experts.
> ```

Secondly, translinguistic apposition never juxtaposes French and English. Likewise, no languages other than Kinyarwanda, French and English are involved. Thirdly, where Kinyarwanda, French and English are concerned, there seems to be a division of labour. As a general rule, Kinyarwanda is juxtaposed to either French or English, as in Examples 6.6 and 6.7 above, with reference to Rwandan traditional / cultural realities and concepts, while French and English are excluded from this area of signification. Finally, in translinguistic apposition on Igihe, there is a preference for the pattern Kinyarwanda–English over the pattern Kinyarwanda–French. In short, different patterns / properties can be observed in translinguistic apposition on Igihe and the proposed account of it as a bilingual interactional practice addresses them all.

6.3   Sociolinguistic grounds for the impossibility of translinguistic apposition

The Common European Framework for Languages makes a distinction between the *multilingualism of societies* and the *plurilingualism of speakers*, whereby it is recognised that, in a multilingual society, members may have differing plurilingual competences (http://www.coe. int/t/dg4/linguistic/Source/LE_texts_Source/EducPlurInter-Projet_en.pdf; last accessed 18 May 2016). This distinction societal multilingualism / individual plurilingualism nicely captures the situation in Rwanda. As we have seen, at the societal level, Rwanda recognises three official languages, namely Kinyarwanda, French and English (Constitution of the Republic of Rwanda, article 5). This official multilingualism is a result of a complex history (pre-colonial, colonial and post-colonial) that space does not allow me to detail here (see Gafaranga et al., 2013, for a summary). A crucial period in this history is the 1990–4 civil war. The war pitted against each other the then government and a rebel group, largely recruited from exiles who had left the country because of earlier bouts of political unrest since the late 1950s, and spearheaded by refugees formerly based in Uganda. The war ended when the rebels defeated the government forces. This turn of events led to the massive return of former refugees and the creation of new ones. This period is significant linguistically because, before the war, Rwanda was officially bilingual in French and Kinyarwanda and, after it, it became trilingual in Kinyarwanda, French and English. The current trend is for the country to become bilingual in Kinyarwanda and English, after dropping French.[6]

At the individual level, Rwandans are diversely competent in the official languages. To denote these differing competences, Rwandans use the language-based categories 'Francophone' and 'Anglophone'. The category 'Francophone' mostly comprises Rwandans who were in the country before the war and a few who returned from French-speaking countries (such as Burundi and Congo). As for Anglophones, they are former refugees from English-speaking countries, mostly Uganda. The social linguistic categories 'Francophone' / 'Anglophone' can easily be extended to the Rwandan diaspora as, following the war, some have settled in English-speaking countries (e.g. Uganda, Kenya, the UK and the USA), while others have settled in French-speaking countries, mostly France and Belgium.

However, the categories 'Francophone' and 'Anglophone' are grossly reductionist and do not adequately capture the actual reality on the ground. To start with, note the significant absence of the category 'Rwandophone', an absence which indexes the fact that every Rwandan is assumed to be proficient in Kinyarwanda. In addition, the education system in place between 1994 and 2009 might have rounded, but not completely removed, the linguistic differences among those who attended it. During this period, a bilingual education system was implemented whereby there were French-medium schools and English-medium schools, with children compulsorily taking the other language as a subject. Finally, in Rwanda as in many other multilingual countries, the languages are not kept separate and everybody is exposed to them all, although differently. In other words, in reality, Rwandans have many and diverse plurilingual competences in the three official languages, although, in terms of numbers, the balance definitely tilts in favour of monolingualism in Kinyarwanda. According to some reports, over 95% of the population can speak Kinyarwanda, up to 5% of the population are bilingual in Kinyarwanda and French, a tiny minority of 3% are bilingual in Kinyarwanda and English, and an even tinier minority are trilingual in Kinyarwanda, French and English (Samuelson and Freedman, 2010). Finally, it is worth noting that some Rwandans have access to additional languages (e.g. Swahili, Russian, Chinese, etc.) due to their particular histories, education for example. Briefly, the reality is one of diverse plurilingual competences, ranging from monolingualism in Kinyarwanda to trilingualism in Kinyarwanda, French and English, via degrees of bilingualism in Kinyarwanda and French, and of bilingualism in Kinyarwanda and English, and occasionally other additional languages. It is precisely because of this diversity that the issue of the possibility of translanguaging in MHR texts in Rwanda arises.

6.4   Theoretical grounds for the apparent impossibility of translinguistic apposition

In a discussion of 'language alternation in writing', Sebba (2002) offers a typology of texts based on the degree to which language is 'standardised and controlled', as in Figure 6.1. Based on these criteria, texts in Igihe can be seen as fitting into the category of MHR texts: they are published and intended for a general and anonymous public. At the institutional level, they are produced by a registered company, namely Igihe Ltd. Even when they originate from members of the public, as is normal practice for multi-author blogs, they are 'professionally' edited.[7]

Sebba (2002) observes what he calls the 'ideology of the standard' and comments that it is strongest in the case of MHR texts on two levels: namely, the level of spelling and that of language choice. Regarding language choice, he writes:

> In printed texts, monolingualism is the norm and the great majority of texts are written in a single language. Even where texts are produced bilingually, for example for official purposes, this in practice always means that two (or more) separate monolingual texts are created, one of which is a complete or partial translation of the other. (http://www.ling.lancs.ac.uk/staff/mark/vigo/regspace; accessed 19 March 2013)

Elsewhere, Sebba speaks of *hegemonic monolingualism*, 'an ideology that legitimates only texts that conform to the norms of a single (usually

Regime	Writing types (examples)	Institutional order	Readership
Most highly regulated	Texts for publication	Publishing/ journalism, etc.	General public
	Texts for circulation (memos, business letters, etc.)	Business/ employment	Colleagues/ competitors
↓	'School' writing	School	Teachers
	Poetry, 'literary' writing	Publishing	Identified readership
Partly regulated	Personal letters	Not institutional	Self/intimates
	Private diaries	Not institutional	Self/intimates
↓	Personal memos (notes, lists)	Not institutional	Self/associates
	Electronic media (e-mail, chat rooms)	Not institutional	Self/in-group
Least regulated	Fanzines, 'samizdat'	Oppositional	In-group
	Graffiti	Oppositional	In-group/ General public

Figure 6.1   Regulation regimes for different texts (www.ling.lancs.ac.uk/ staff/mark/vigo/regspace; last accessed 19 March 2013)

named and standardised) language', and finds its influence to be 'exerted particularly strongly on printed texts which are produced for public consumption' (2013: 100). Based on these observations, translinguistic apposition on Igihe can be seen as impossible in principle.

However, Sebba is quick to note that there may be 'exceptions, and different norms apply in some language communities, allowing for the production – routinely or occasionally, depending on the community – of multilingual texts' (2013: 100). Additionally, he remarks that 'the internet has produced a large additional space, relatively free from normative constraints, in which speakers can practise multilingualism in written, computer-mediated communication' (2013: 100). These additional observations, together with the facts noted earlier about Igihe (being online, its overall organisation in three language versions and the practice of translinguistic apposition), call for closer scrutiny. Particularly important here is the matter of being produced online, a fact which, if taken literally, may lead to the view that Igihe is only 'partly regulated' and 'free from normative constraints'. However, as shown in the paragraphs below, the linguistic reality in the paper does not support this view.

Sebba (2013) identifies two major multilingual text-types, namely *parallel texts* and *complementary texts*, based on three criteria: language-spatial relationship, language-content relationship and linguistic mixing. At the overall level, Igihe meets the language-spatial relationship of a parallel text since it is published in three language versions, but it fails to meet the language-content relationship of a parallel text. Indeed, not everything published in one language is published in the others and, if something is published in all three versions, the three versions need not be published simultaneously. That is, the three versions are not mere translations of one another. For example, at the point of writing (17 February 2014 at 14:00), a story on the split within an opposition party (Rwanda National Congress) was heading the news in the Kinyarwanda version, but was only secondary news in the French version and was not even featuring (yet) in the English version. A story featuring the President's speech on healthcare was headline news in the English version but was not even appearing as secondary news either in Kinyarwanda or in French. That is to say, at the overall level, Igihe has features of both parallel texts and complementary texts.

Two comments are worth highlighting. Firstly, the fact that the paper appears in three language versions, even if the versions are not complete translations of each other, does not mean that Igihe is unregulated. Indeed, according to Sebba (2002), MHR texts may consist of 'separate monolingual texts (. . .) one of which is a (. . .) partial translation of the other'. Secondly, it is important to note the assumption about readers' plurilingual status that the overall organisation of Igihe entails. According to Sebba (2013), a parallel text-type assumes monolingual readers, hence equivalent content in all the languages involved, and a complementary text-type assumes a bilingual readership, as what is said in one language is not necessarily repeated in the other (2013: 109). Given the distribution of content on Igihe, as briefly discussed above, it is easy to see that, at the overall level, a Kinyarwanda–French–English trilingual readership is assumed. Readers' plurilingual competence is assumed to be such that they can access the texts in any of the three languages. Trilingual competence is assumed to be standard among readers. The question is: where does this assumption come from? How can this assumption of trilingual competence be seen as warranted?

While the criterion of language-spatial relationship and that of language-content relationship can be examined at the macro level of the paper as a whole, that of linguistic mixing can be examined only at the level of individual texts. The question here is whether specific articles on Igihe are multilingual or not and, if they are, whether they can still be seen as regulated. In many cases, texts are monolingual in the sense that they do not contain any instance of language alternation. Clearly, in these cases, the monolingualism norm applies and nothing indicates that the texts are not regulated. Could the same norm be seen as still applying in the cases where translinguistic apposition is observed? Alternatively, can translinguistic apposition be seen as a challenge to hegemonic monolingualism? Could texts containing translinguistic apposition be seen as being not very regulated?

CS scholars have shown that, in multilingual discourse, two types of language alternation can be identified. In some cases, the otherness of language alternation is oriented to as such and, in some other cases, it is not (Auer, 1984; Gafaranga, 2007b). In the latter case, researchers speak of the *bilingual medium* (Gafaranga, 2007b; see also Chapter 2 in this book), of *unmarked code-switching* (Myers-Scotton, 1993b) and, more generally, of code-mixing. In the former, the term *language alternation as deviance from the medium* (Gafaranga, 2007b: 148) seems appropriate. In suggesting that language alternation is in principle impossible in MHR texts, Sebba (2002) does not take account of the above distinction, but I would like to argue that it is very significant. In the case at hand, trans-linguistic apposition will be seen as a challenge to hegemonic monolingualism, and therefore as impossible in principle, only if the otherness of language choice is not oriented to as such. But if language alternation is an instance of deviance from a monolingual medium, it cannot be seen as a challenge to the same medium with reference to which it is identified. Instead, in this case, translanguaging can be seen as reinforcing the monolingual norm, from which it derives its value.

Available evidence indicates that, in translinguistic apposition on Igihe, the otherness of language choice is oriented to as such. Consider the following two instances of what we might call *other-language-ness formulation*. In general, the term 'formulation', as used in conversation analysis, is when participants describe and / or name the activity they are involved in (Garfinkel and Sacks, 1970). In line with this, other-language-ness formulation can be understood as when participants explicitly indicate that a particular item deviates from the on-going medium, notably by naming its origin.

Extract 6.8 (Un Monument de la culture rwandaise en plein effondrement, Igihe, 12 August 2011)

Ce jeudi, autour de 17 h, à l'hôpital Roi Fayçal, Sentore Athanase débarque sur une chaise roulante dans un état que seul un *homme intègre* (**imfura en Kinyarwanda**) peut supporter.

This Thursday, at around 17:00, at the Roi Fayçal
Hospital, Sentore Athanase arrived in a wheelchair in
a state that only a man of character ('man of character' in Kinyarwanda) can bear.

Extract 6.9 (2012: Ibihugu byaje ku isonga mu bukire ku isi, Igihe, 19
April 2013)

Ubundi iyo bagiye kureba ibihugu bikize kurusha
ibindi bareba *umusaruro wabyo ku mwaka*, ibyo bita
mu ndimi z'amahanga ***Produit Intérieur Brut*** (PIB) /
Gross Domestic Product (GDP), ungana n'umusaruro wose
w'igihugu mu nzego zose ukuyemo igishoro batanze.

In establishing the relative wealth of countries, they
look at their annual income, what they call in foreign
languages Gross Domestic Product (PIB / GDP), which
amounts to the difference between a country's total
production and its investment.

In Extract 6.8, the writer formulates the other-language-ness of *imfura*,
referring to it as Kinyarwanda. Likewise, in Extract 9.9, the writer formulates the other-language-ness of *produit intérieur brut* and *gross domestic
product*, describing them as coming from *indimi z'amahanga* ('foreign
languages').[8] The point about formulation, as Heritage (1985) and Drew
(2003) have noted, is that it is rare, but significant, in discourse. That
is, in discourse, activities are often accomplished without being formulated as such. In the above instances, for example, other-language-ness
formulation could have been avoided and the result would have been
what, in the on-going discussion, I am referring to as translinguistic
apposition. Conversely, each instance of translinguistic apposition can
easily be 'other-language-ness formulated'. Therefore, it can safely be
concluded that, in translinguistic apposition, the other-language-ness of
the juxtaposed item is oriented to as such.

   Further evidence of other-language-ness in translinguistic apposition
can be found in situations such as Extract 6.4 above and Extract 6.10
below.

Extract 6.10 (Urwanda rugiye gushyira ku isoko ry'iBurayi impapuro
z'agaciro milioni 400$, Igihe, 17 April 2013)

U Rwanda rurateganya gushyira *impapuro z'agaciro-
faranga* (**Treasury Bonds**) ka miliyoni 400 z'amadolari

```
y'Amerika ku isoko ry'imari i Buraya, kugira ngo
rukomeze guteza imbere ubukungu bwarwo.

---------------------------

Rwanda is going to issue treasury bonds (treasury
bonds) worth $400 million for the European market in
order to support its development.
```

In both extracts, the writer has to express a reality which is not very common in the Rwandan context ('steno dactylographer' in Extract 6.4 and 'treasury bonds' in Extract 6.10) and, therefore, one for which no Kinyarwanda expression exists (yet). To overcome the difficulty, he / she coins a new expression and, recognising the possibility that it might not be understood, back-translates it into English. The fact that the writers went to the extent of coining new Kinyarwanda expressions, even though they had access to the right expressions in English, demonstrates their orientation to the other-language-ness of the English expressions. Note that, in less 'regulated' situations, such as informal conversation, the items would typically be inserted, the process leading to a bilingual medium.

A third piece of evidence can be found in situations such as Extract 6.11. In the absence of an original Kinyarwanda word for 'roundabout', Kinyarwanda has borrowed and integrated the French word *rond point* as *rompuwe*. In the extract, the original French word is appositioned to this French-origin Kinyarwanda word. Clearly, were it not for the regulated nature of the discourse, the French word would have been inserted.

Extract 6.11 (Ibintu 20 byahindutse mu Rwanda mu myaka makumyabiri ishize, Igihe, 14 April 2014)

```
Ikindi kandi ni uko hari ahabaga feruje, ariko ubu
zikaba zarakuweho zigasimbuzwa rompuwe (Rond point /
Roundabout)

---------------------------

The other thing is that, where there used to be traffic
lights, sometimes you now find roundabouts (roundabout/
roundabout).
```

Briefly, in translinguistic apposition, the other-language-ness of the appositioned item is oriented to as such, whether it is formulated or not. Therefore, translinguistic apposition cannot be seen as a challenge to hegemonic monolingualism and, as a result, it cannot be used as evidence that the texts in which it appears are unregulated. All in all, Igihe is a multilingual paper with monolingual articles, whether or not they contain instances of translinguistic apposition. That is, Igihe and specific texts within it demonstrably belong to the category of MHR texts. More importantly, as translinguistic apposition is not a challenge to hegemonic monolingualism, the issue of its possibility at the theoretical level dissipates. The theoretical impossibility of translinguistic apposition is only an apparent one.

6.5 Translinguistic apposition as a context-shaped practice

As the sections above show, the actual issue translinguistic apposition raises is a sociolinguistic one. The issue arises because of a potential clash between a defining requirement of the text-type and the reality on the ground. The practice assumes that competence in Kinyarwanda, French and English is standard among the readership (Section 6.4), while, in reality, no such standard competence exists. As we have seen, the reality is one of a great diversity of plurilingual competences. In reality, as discussed above, trilingual competence in Kinyarwanda, French and English can be found only among a very small minority of Rwandans. In turn, this diversity of competences, particularly the lack of competence in all three languages, leads to the question of how translanguagers can be confident that their meanings will be understood as intended. A possible counter-claim here could be that the problem does not even arise, as translinguistic apposition is a mere case of what Eastman and Stein (1993) call *language display*. In language display, competence in the switched-to language is not required, as language alternation serves only a symbolic function. However, this claim is contradicted by *deviant instances* (see 'deviant case analysis' in Heritage, 1984), such as Extract 6.10. As we have seen, Rwanda has issued its first 'treasury bonds'. In reporting the event, the writer coined the expression *impapuro z'agaciro-faranga* for the reasons we have noted and juxtaposed the English equivalent to it. Right after, a flurry of comments followed, calling for the term *treasury bond* to be explained, until a reader came up with the following explanation:

Extract 6.12 (a comment from a reader, Igihe, 17 April 2013)

```
Ibi biranyereka ko Economics ari ubumenyi budapfa
kwisukirwa. Abantu bose ntibashoboye gusobanukirwa na
Bond icyo aricyo na logic behind it. Bond ni urupap-
uro rugurishwa na Central Bank cyangwa indi company
ku buryo bwo kwaka inguzanyo (loan) kuko abantu baru-
gura batanze cash (liquidity) maze Leta cg iyo company
```

ikabona amafaranga iba ikoresha mu *igihe ruzarangirira* (**maturity**) kitaragera ngo Leta cg <u>company</u> yishyure <u>cash</u> *yakiriye igurisha* (**principal**) n'*inyungu ziya-herekeje* (**underlying interest**). Aha rero kugirango izo <u>bonds</u> zigurwe, Leta cg <u>company</u> zigomba kuba zifitiwe *icyizere* (**reputation or trust**) ku isoko mpuzamahanga ry'imari, niyo mpamvu habaho <u>Credit Rating System</u> ikorwa na <u>Standard</u>.

This shows me that <u>Economics</u> is not a cup of tea for everyone. Not everybody has been able to understand what bond means and the <u>logic behind</u> it. A bond is a piece of paper sold by a central bank or any other company by way of securing a loan (<u>loan</u>). People buy it in cash (<u>liquidity</u>) and, thereby, the state or company gets the money to spend until the time comes (<u>maturity</u>) for the state or company to reimburse the money it received (<u>principal</u>) and the interest that it has accrued (<u>underlying interest</u>). For those bonds to sell, the state or company must be trusted (<u>reputa-tion or trust</u>) on the international monetary market, and that's the reason why you have the Credit Rating System by Standard.

The fact that, on this occasion, readers have explicitly orientated to the referential meaning of the appositioned item confirms that, even in the many cases where they do not, they potentially could. Also, the fact that, on this occasion, translinguistic apposition has failed confirms that the success of the strategy cannot be taken for granted and therefore that the issue of its possibility is a real one. In other words, the interactional phenomenon at hand cannot be reduced to mere language display. In the following sections, a two-step account of the possibility of trans-linguistic apposition at the sociolinguistic level is proposed.

6.5.1 Language choice and 'ascribed' linguistic competence

Sebba (2013) highlights the limits of current models of spoken CS (see Chapter 2) for the study of CS in spoken texts. Two major sources of difficulties are identified, namely the interactive nature of spoken discourse and its sequential organisation versus the absence thereof in written discourse (2013: 109). In other words, in spoken discourse, meanings are negotiated interactively and understandings revealed, confirmed or rejected in the sequences of participants' actions. This possibility of negotiation is unavailable in the case of written discourse, especially 'where one or both of the interacting parties is anonymous' (2013: 109). It is precisely because of this absence of the possibility of local negotiation in MHR texts that standard practices, including at the level of language choice, must be adopted. That is to say, the need for the standard is not merely ideological; it can also be practical. On this count alone, current models of CS can be anticipated to be inappropriate for translinguistic apposition.

There are also problems inherent in models of CS relative to the Rwandan sociolinguistic situation as described above. A running assumption in current models of CS is what I might call the *language competence fallacy*. This is the idea that, in order to alternate languages, participants must be competent in the languages involved. Along these lines, Meeuwis and Blommaert (1998) comment that current models of CS imply 'that the code-switching speakers *actually* "know" (the) languages (involved)' (1998: 77; my italics). It is in recognition of this language competence fallacy that, as Sebba (2002: 112–13) reports, the concept of *code-switching* is increasingly challenged and alternative ones (e.g. *translanguaging* (García, 2009), *plurilingual languaging* (Jørgensen, 2008) and *metrolingualism* (Otsuji and Pennycook, 2009)) are gaining increased currency.

However, even though models of CS cannot be imported wholesale to account for translanguaging practices in written texts, they cannot be rejected wholesale either (Sebba, 2013). In the case of translinguistic apposition, some of the understandings developed in studies of CS can be usefully drawn upon. Top among these is Auer's view that

> bilingualism is (not) something inside the speaker's head, but (rather) a
> displayed feature of participants' everyday behaviour (. . .) bilingualism is
> a predicate *ascribed to and by participants* on the basis of visible, inspectable
> behaviour. (1988 / 2000: 169; emphasis added)

The same view is shared by Gafaranga (2001), Torras (2005), Torras and Gafaranga (2002), Cashman (2005) and others, according to whom bilingualism is a *social identity* (Antaki and Widdicombe, 1998: 2). Following the ethnomethodological tradition, these authors argue that, in order to talk, bilingual participants categorise themselves and one another either as monolingual in language A or in language B, or as bilingual in languages A and B. Furthermore, they argue that this ascription and categorisation need not reflect participants' actual competence in those languages.

Evidence can easily be found in support of this view. Consider Extract 6.13 below, an instance of what one might call *self-initiated medium self-repair* (see Chapter 5). In the extract, participant D has held his addressee not to be competent in English and proceeded to repair its use, without any prior enquiry as to whether the addressee really and truly cannot understand what is said in this language.

Extract 6.13

```
1. D:  Ufite homework- devoir
2. A:  Ahaaa! Ni ikibazo gikomeye

--------------------------

1. D:  Do you have a homework— homework
2. A:  Ahaaa! It's a big problem
```

Also consider Extract 6.14 below. The interaction started in Kinyarwanda and then switched to French. In turn 1, B uses Kinyarwanda in a first pair part of an adjacency pair. In 2, C provides a relevant second pair part, indicating thereby that, for all practical purposes, she is competent in Kinyarwanda. However, she delivers her contribution in French. In 3, B moves from his previous use of Kinyarwanda to French. Therefore the switch to French by B cannot be explained in terms of C's objective and demonstrated lack of competence in Kinyarwanda.

Extract 6.14

```
1. B:  Ni nde wakwigishije?
2. C:  Moi toute seule
3. B:  Toute seule?
4. C:  Les copines qui m'ont montrée

--------------------------

1. B:  Who taught you to do it?
2. C:  (I learned) all by myself
3. B:  (you learned) all by yourself?
4. C:  Some friends showed me (how to do it)
```

Extract 6.15 is even more interesting.

Extract 6.15

```
1. A:  noneho rero nka bariya b' impunzi ukuntu bigenda
       (.) babagira ba (.) a a amashuri hano ni privé
       quoi (.) ni privé mbega (.) kuburyo rero kugi-
       rango aze muri iyi université agomba kwishyura
```

2. B: umh
3. A: *mais comme* nta mafaranga afite ay yatse *bourse le*
        (.) babyita **local government**
4. B   umh
5. A: **local authority** *donc* ni nkaaa
6. B: ni nka *municipalité*
7. A: ni nka *municipalité c'est ça* (.) *municipalité*
        yahano niyo yamuhaye *bourse*

----

1. A: refugees like him are (.) schools here are
        private (.) they are *private* so that he must pay
        to study at this *university*
2. B: umh
3. A: *but as* he doesn't have money he has had to apply
        for a *grant* from the (.) they call it local
        government
4. B: umh
5. A: local authority well it's likeee
6. B: it's like a *municipality*
7. A: that's right it's like a *municipality* (.) he got
        a *grant* from the local *municipality*

In the extract, A runs into difficulty finding the word for what he wants to say – namely, *municipalité* – and draws on English to signal to his co-participant exactly what it is he is having problems with. In turn 6, B produces the repair and in 7 A ratifies it. In using English and hoping that it will help get around the *self-initiated-other-repair problem* (Gafaranga, 2012: 511 and Chapter 5), A holds B to be objectively competent in English. And in providing the repair, B confirms this competence for all practical purposes. However, in turn 5, A undertakes to repair the very same choice of English. By so doing, A holds B, and indeed himself, not to be bilingual in English. In so many words, A can be paraphrased as having said that, here and now, we are not doing being competent in English, even though objectively we are. Briefly, bilingualism is not what people really are, but rather what they hold each other to be for the purpose of on-going interaction. Language choice is accountable for, not in terms of actual competence in languages X, Y and Z, but in terms of the linguistic competence participants ascribe to one another for the purpose of the interaction at hand. If this view of what it means to be bilingual is adopted, the issue of the possibility of translinguistic apposition on Igihe is quickly resolved: writers hold their readers to be competent in Kinyarwanda, French and English. Whether they actually are is beside the point.

However, as it is, this account of the possibility of translinguistic apposition leaves one important issue unresolved. The account allows for any language to participate in the structure. According to the explanation so far, translinguistic apposition can involve any language, the only deciding factor being the writer's own plurilingual status. That is to say, under this explanation, it would be possible for writers to draw on their own plurilingual competence independently of their readers' competence. Under such a view, translinguistic apposition would indeed be seen as a case of language display. The limit of this view has already been demonstrated. In addition, the view that any language can participate in the structure is not supported by the data. In the data, only Kinyarwanda, French and English are ever involved in translinguistic apposition. Despite my best efforts, I have not been able to locate a single instance of translinguistic apposition involving a language other than Kinyarwanda, French or English. In the sections below, I argue that the empirical fact that only Kinyarwanda, French and English are involved in translinguistic apposition is accounted for by linking the macro level language policy and the micro level language choice practice.

6.5.2   Macro language policies as contexts for micro language choice practices

It is almost a truism to say that language choice acts are context-embedded. To understand the context-embeddedness of translinguistic apposition, the notion of *context* itself must be clearly understood. A useful starting point is the following observation by Goodwin and Duranti:

> When the issue of context is raised it is typically assumed that the *focal event* cannot be properly understood (. . .), unless one looks *beyond the event itself to other phenomena* (for example cultural setting, speech situation, shared background assumptions) within which the event is embedded (. . .) The context is thus a *frame* (Goffman, 1974) that surrounds the event being examined and provides *resources for its appropriate interpretation*. (1992: 3; emphasis added)

In the observation it is highlighted that any idea of context implies a focal event, i.e. the phenomenon being investigated. Without a focal event, there is no context. In the extract, it is also emphasised that the context consists of phenomena other than the focal event itself. Finally, it is stressed that the context is a resource for the interpretation of the focal event. This last point must be explored further. Given a focal event, phenomena outside it are potentially infinite. However, out of that potential infinity, only phenomena contributing to the appropriate interpretation of the focal event are retained as its context. In this respect, Drew and Heritage (1992), Heritage and Clayman (2010), and especially Schegloff (1992) speak of the *relevance of context*.

A closer look at the notion of context has revealed two possible ways of thinking about context, respectively termed a *bucket view* and a *context-renewing view* (Drew and Heritage, 1992: 21). In the bucket theory, the context is seen as static and independent of the focal event. The context-renewing view, on the other hand, holds that discourse is shaped by the (relevant) context and that, in turn, through discourse, the relevant context is revealed and renewed. In other words, through discourse, the relevant context is talked into being. Schegloff (1992) speaks of the *procedural consequentiality of context*. This context-renewing view of context has been adopted in a variety of studies, those of institutional talk in particular (see Heritage and Clayman, 2010: 20–33, for a succinct review). Other studies have related language choice and specific sociolinguistic contexts. For example, Gafaranga (2010) and Gafaranga (2011) show how language shift, as a sociolinguistic context, shapes participants' talk. Both studies investigate language choice among Rwandans in Belgium, where language shift is reported to be taking place from Kinyarwanda–French bilingualism to monolingualism in French. This sociolinguistic situation is demonstrated to lead to the adoption of specific conversational practices, namely *medium request* (2010) and *transition space medium repair* (2011). Conversely, I argue, by adopting these specific practices, members of the community talk language shift into being. Building on the view that language choice practices are shaped by the sociolinguistic contexts in which they take place and, therefore, that through the very same language choice practices, relevant sociolinguistic contexts are talked into being, it may be argued that the practice of translinguistic apposition, as observed on Igihe, is shaped by the Rwandan sociolinguistic context and, conversely, through translinguistic apposition, that sociolinguistic context is written into being. A convenient way of referring to this sociolinguistic situation is in terms of the Rwandan macro language policy.

6.5.3 Translinguistic apposition and the Rwandan macro language policy

Spolsky (2004) has convincingly argued that language policy can be seen as comprising three components: language management, language ideologies and beliefs, and language practices. According to Spolsky, *language management* (or *declared language policy*, Shohamy, 2006) refers to 'the formulation or proclamation of an explicit plan or policy, usually but not necessarily written in a formal document, about language use' (2004: 11). In this respect, the Constitution of the Republic of Rwanda (2003, article 5) states:

> The national language is Kinyarwanda.
> The official languages are Kinyarwanda, French and English.

This macro language policy shapes the practice of translinguistic apposition on Igihe and is shaped by it in many ways. First of all, as we have seen, the overall organisation of the paper and the local practice of translinguistic apposition, in contradiction with the reality on the ground, are based on the assumption that competence in Kinyarwanda, French and English is standard among readers. As we have seen, in actual fact, Rwandans' plurilingual competences are diverse and only a tiny minority can actually claim trilingual competence in Kinyarwanda, French and English. An empirical question was therefore felt to be how this assumption of trilingual competence among readers can be seen as warranted.

To address this question, we begin by noting that Kinyarwanda, French and English are the very same languages that the constitution recognises as official. The assumption that citizens standardly know these languages can easily be understood by reference to the language rights literature. According to language rights theorists, it is a 'civic duty to be competent in the (official) language' (Rubio-Marin, 2003: 71). Evidence for this civic duty is found in practices such as the requirement for immigrants applying for naturalisation to demonstrate competence in the official language through language tests. In other words, given the Rwandan macro policy, readers of Igihe, as competent members of Rwandan society, can warrantably be assumed to be competent in its official languages. Conversely, given the same macro policy limiting the official languages to Kinyarwanda, French and English, citizens cannot be warrantably assumed to know any other language, even though, as individuals, they in fact may (see Section 6.2). The macro language policy shapes and constrains the practice of translinguistic apposition. In turn, given the routine nature of the practice, by redeploying it for yet another first time in specific instances, writers write the constitution into being. In praxis terms, Kinyarwanda, French and English are the official languages of Rwanda because they can warrantably be used to accomplish specific interactional activities, in this case translinguistic apposition.

Although Rwandans can justifiably be assumed to be competent in the country's official languages, the constitution does not actually specify whether competence should be had in one of them, in some of them or in all of them. In the absence of any detail, each institution has to develop its own interpretation. For example, the available evidence is that the Rwandan Parliament has adopted the view that Rwandans are either Francophones or Anglophones. As a result, as reported in Gafaranga et al. (2013), texts of draft bills take the form of parallel texts (Sebba, 2013) and are compulsorily available in Kinyarwanda, French and English. Recently, the National Bank of Rwanda issued a new 500 Rwandan franc note with parallel texts in Kinyarwanda and English (Figure 6.2). Through this action, only competence in Kinyarwanda and / or in English is assumed.

In view of its language choice practices, Igihe can be seen as having interpreted the macro policy as implying competence in all three languages. At the macro level, as we have seen, Igihe has adopted the structure of complementary texts (Sebba, 2013). A number of observations at the micro level of translinguistic apposition can be accounted for along the same lines. In many cases, Kinyarwanda is juxtaposed with one other language. In other cases, as in Extract 6.5, consecutive structures may involve different languages. And there are even situations where all three languages are involved in the same structure, as in extracts 6.16 and 6.17.

Extract 6.16 (Ninde ufite uburenganzira bwo gusaba pansiyo y'ubusaza, Igihe, 2 July 2014)

Igihe noneho umukozi asabye amafaranga ye y'izabukuru atarageza ku myaka 15 y'ubwiteganyirize, ahabwa *amafaranga y'ingunga imwe (**allocation unique / <u>lumpsum</u>**).

When an employer requests their pension before they have completed 15 years of service, they get a lump sum (lump sum / lump sum).

Extract 6.17 (Uburundi bwibutse Perezida Ntaryamira waguye mu ndege ya Habyarimana, Igihe, 8 April 2014)

Imihango yo kwibuka uyu wahoze ari umukuru w'igihugu yaranzwe n'igitambo cya misa muri katedarale ya Regina Mundi ndetse no gushyira indabo ku mva ya Nyakwigendera ariko nta *mbwirwaruhame* (***discours* / speech**) yigeze itangwa.

Remembrance ceremonies for this former head of state consisted of a church service at the Regina Mundi cathedral and the laying of flowers at his tomb but no speeches (speech / speech) were pronounced.

Figure 6.2   New 500 Rwandan franc note (www.igihe.com, 24 September 2013; last accessed 17 June 2014)

In short, on Igihe, the Rwandan macro policy is given a specific inter-pretation, i.e. is written into being.

We have observed a division of labour among the three official lan-guages of Rwanda in translinguistic apposition. While Kinyarwanda is switched to in the context of Rwandan traditional and cultural realities, French and English are excluded from this area. A binary system with or without cultural reality seems to be at work. This functional distri-bution of the Rwandan official languages in translinguistic apposition is indexical of the macro policy. According to the Rwandan constitu-tion, Kinyarwanda is the national language. At the ideological level, Kinyarwanda is strongly associated with the Rwandan culture and national identity (see Gafaranga et al., 2013, for a detailed discussion). On the other hand, French and English are associated with technology, science and modernity. Indeed, one of the reasons evoked for adopting these languages in a country which, for all practical purposes, is mono-lingual is that Kinyarwanda is not developed enough to express these realities fully. According to Spolsky, such 'beliefs about language and language use' are an important component of a language policy (2004: 5). Other authors have spoken of the *ideological* or *perceived language policy* (Shohamy, 2006). In translinguistic apposition, this ideological dimension of the Rwandan macro language policy is renewed through the functional differentiation of the languages involved. This aspect of the Rwandan macro policy also accounts for the fact that, as mentioned earlier, switching from Kinyarwanda to either French or English is far more common than the other way round. Kinyarwanda needs these languages more than they need it.

The same binary system with or without cultural reality leads to yet another aspect of the Rwandan macro language policy and, in turn, explains yet another feature of translinguistic apposition. This is the fact that, in Rwanda, while French and English are seen as complementing Kinyarwanda, between themselves they are seen as duplicating each other. To understand this, we can refer to Fishman's (1967 / 2000) argu-ment that functional differentiation is a prerequisite for two languages to exist side by side. While Rwanda had been bilingual in Kinyarwanda and French as a result of its colonial past, English was recognised for the first time as having some role to play in Rwandan multilingualism as part of the Arusha Peace Accord (1993), an accord which was meant to resolve the then on-going civil war. Recall that the war opposed the Rwandan Government and a rebel movement spearheaded by Anglophone refugees. However, the accord provided that English would be allowed only for three years, during which time the returnees would learn French. That is to say, the negotiators as policy-makers did not envision a situation where French and English would co-exist on a permanent basis. However, history has proved them wrong and English never went away. Rather, today, as we see below, there is evidence that it is displacing French, presumably because, the two serving the same function and English being 'associated with the dominant drift of social forces' (Fishman, 2000: 87), they cannot exist side by side. Briefly, the sociolinguistic structure of Rwandan multilingualism can be represented as in Figure 6.3, meant to capture the crucial fact that French and English are not in contact but in parallel with each other. This aspect of the Rwandan macro language policy shapes and is shaped by the practice of translinguistic apposition on Igihe. As mentioned earlier, while cases of translinguistic apposition with the patterns Kinyarwanda–French and Kinyarwanda–English are common, French and English are never juxtaposed to each other. Also, as Extracts 6.11, 6.15 and 6.16 show, French and English can actually co-occur in the same instance and be accomplishing the same job relative to Kinyarwanda, i.e. duplicating each other.

Finally, as we have noted, in translinguistic apposition, the pattern Kinyarwanda–English appears to be more common than the pattern Kinyarwanda–French and this too can be accounted for. The constitution recognises three official languages but, in reality, the influence of French is fast and noticeably decreasing. Language displacement is taking place in favour of English. For example, the medium of instruction has already changed from French to English in all Rwandan schools (Samuelson and Freedman, 2010). It is increasingly becoming acceptable to omit French in official documents (see the newest 500 Rwandan franc bank note, Figure 6.3). Even when the three languages are still co-present, there is a tendency to push French physically to a third position, as in the letterhead shown in Figure 6.4, in contradiction with the constitution, which suggests it to be the second official language (Gafaranga et al., 2013: 321). In other words, there is a gap between the declared policy, which recognises three official languages, and the *practised policy* (Bonacina-Pugh, 2012; Papageorgiou, 2012), which in effect sidelines one of them. This aspect of the Rwandan macro language

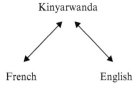

Figure 6.3   The Rwandan sociolinguistic structure

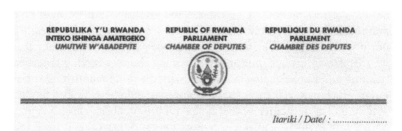

Figure 6.4   Letterhead of the Rwandan Parliament

policy shows at the level of the practice of translinguistic apposition, i.e. shapes it, through a reduced presence of French compared to English. French is becoming less of a resource for local interactional practices such as translinguistic apposition.

6.6   Summary and conclusion

This third illustrative case study of bilingualism as interactional practices has focused on translinguistic apposition in MHR texts in Rwanda. Three levels at which this practice can be seen as different from the previous two can be highlighted. Firstly, the practice of translinguistic apposition is different from the previous two in that it is context-specific. Secondly, it is different in that, unlike the other two, it was observed in written texts. Thirdly, unlike the other two case studies previously included, the present case started, not from any previous reports of the practice, but from empirical observation of the data. Despite these differences, however, the same methodological orientation was adopted and it led to a clear understanding of the practice. As a starting point, a hitherto unknown phenomenon was noticed. However, as indicated earlier, even here, the role of previous research was significant, as the practice was noted only because it seemed to run counter to expectations, previously announced in the literature, that language alternation is impossible in MHR texts (Sebba, 2002, 2013). Furthermore, the practice was felt to be impossible in principle on practical sociolinguistic grounds. It assumed that competence in Kinyarwanda, French and English was standard among Rwandans while, in reality, it is not. Therefore, it was felt that an account of the practice should resolve these two issues.

In a second step, a corpus of data was gathered and scrutinised, this leading to the identification of different patterns in the practice. Observations were formulated regarding the direction of language switches, the relative frequency of specific patterns of switches, the functional distribution of the different patterns and so on. Therefore, in developing an account of the practice, the chapter addressed the general issues of the possibility of translinguistic apposition, as well as the specific issues raised by these observations. Notably, the chapter demonstrated that, at the theoretical level, the issue of the possibility of translinguistic apposition does not actually arise, as the other--language-ness of the switched-to items is oriented as such. As for the issues resulting from the specific sociolinguistic context of Rwanda, the chapter demonstrated that they all are resolved by linking the macro-level language policy and the micro-level interactional practice.

In conclusion, the case study confirms the strength of the methodology proposed for the investigation of bilingualism as interactional practices (Chapter 3). The methodology is flexible enough to be used in investigating interactional practices in spoken as well as in written interactions. It can be used in describing both context-specific practices and general interactional practices. Also, as other researchers, notably Ricento (2000), have highlighted, a general and current concern in language policy research is the need for clear links between macro- and micro-level analyses. This investigation of translinguistic apposition in MHR texts in Rwanda does exactly that. That is, the chapter contributes to a general concern in language policy research and, to that extent, is mainstreamed.

Notes

1. Italic and bold types are used together to highlight appositive structures. In this chapter, as in the rest of the book, underlining indicates English within the language contrast scheme (see 'Transcription conventions').
2. Umwiherero w'Igihugu is a kind of annual national convention which brings together all the authorities and outlines the general policy guidelines for the country.
3. The term 'paper' will be used throughout this chapter for convenience.
4. To be sure, a Kirundi version exists as well, but will not be included in this discussion for the following reason: not a single case of Kinyarwanda–Kirundi translinguistic apposition was observed. This is not surprising, as Kinyarwanda and Kirundi are mutually intelligible and share the same cultural background. Because of this mutual intelligibility, even if such cases existed, they would not raise the same issues of, in principle, impossibility.
5. Actual ethnographic observation may prove this assumption to be wrong.

6. More is said about this wider sociolinguistic context / policy in Section 6.5.3.
7. Note that Igihe has an explicitly declared policy of 'checking' (editing / censoring) even individual readers' comments.
8. Rwandans commonly refer to French and English as indimi z'amahanga ('foreign languages'), even though they are the country's official languages, in contrast to Kinyarwanda, which is felt to be the proper language of the country.

7 Summary and conclusion

The study of bilingualism, and especially of language alternation, has been undertaken against the background of very negative attitudes towards bilingualism in general and bilingual language use in particular. Language alternation was seen mostly as a sign of lack of competence in either of the languages involved. Speakers took part in CS only because they were unable to sustain a conversation in one or the other of the languages involved. Today, however, the situation has improved a great deal, thanks to the research effort over the last few decades, among other things. Previously seen as a handicap, bilingualism is currently considered, in some quarters at least, as an advantage. From being regarded as a random phenomenon and as a sign of inadequate competence in the languages involved, bilingual language use is currently seen as an interactional resource and as a sign of advanced competence in the languages involved. According to some researchers, language alternation contributes to the negotiation of social relationships in interaction and, for some others, it contributes to the organisation of bilingual talk in interaction. Thus, to put it in a nutshell, given where it all started, the main achievement of the discipline so far is to have more or less successfully challenged previously held assumptions and to have rehabilitated bilingualism. Now that this rehabilitation has largely been achieved, the study of bilingualism, as a discipline, faces an entirely new problem: how can it continue to be relevant and interesting? The overall aim of this book has been to contribute to this important issue that the study of bilingualism faces.

The study of bilingualism can be, and indeed has been throughout its history, undertaken from various disciplinary perspectives (e.g. grammatical perspective, psycholinguistic perspective, socio-interactional perspective, etc.). For practical reasons, this book has focused only on the socio-interactional dimension. In this dimension, language choice and CS are examined as contributing to the organisation of the interaction in which they are observed. At this level, the book has argued that the study of bilingualism should proceed from the specific view that bilingualism consists, not of one homogenous linguistic phenomenon which can be exhausted by one theory, but rather of multiple interactional practices, each of which should be investigated in its own right. Thus, the aim of research, it has been implied, should be, not to write big new theories of bilingualism and of language alternation in particular, but rather to accumulate empirical knowledge about the various and specific interactional practices which involve the use of two or more languages. In this type of work, two kinds of question will be pursued: (1) knowing how a particular practice works and (2) knowing exactly how language choice contributes to it. The assumption behind these two questions is, of course, that there is nothing that bilinguals do interactionally that monolinguals cannot do and that, likewise, there is nothing that monolinguals do that bilinguals cannot do, even though this may mean drawing on both of their languages. The real difference, it is assumed, is at the level of the resources available to them. In that sense, in the book, bilingualism is also viewed as an interactional resource.

The two questions above and the view of bilingualism imply important consequences for the nature of bilingualism studies relative to corresponding disciplines. Traditionally, bilingualism, and CS in particular, have been approached in two different ways. Firstly, studies have drawn on existing theories and knowledge, and have applied them for the purpose of explicating bilingualism phenomena. In this view, the relationship between the study of bilingualism and previous knowledge and theories was seen as unidirectional. Knowledge about bilingualism generated through research was not seen, or at least not explicitly, as feeding back into knowledge about language use in general. For example, one studied language alternation using Conversation Analysis, but the results arrived at were never shown to be of any significance for Conversation Analysis itself. Alternatively, but certainly in a lesser measure, bilingualism was evoked by way of confirming or else disconfirming general linguistic theories. In this case, bilingualism was seen as no more than data. In Gumperz, for example, CS is seen merely as one of the many signalling devices or contextualisation cues available to bilingual speakers. In this book, it has been argued that, in order to continue to be relevant, a bidirectional view of the relationship between the study of bilingualism and general knowledge about interactional practices will have to be adopted. The term 'mainstreaming' has been used. Where a particular interactional practice has already been described in monolingual contexts, its counterpart involving the use of two languages will be approached in such a manner that the understanding developed, at the same time, draws on that previous knowledge and contributes back to it. And where an interactional practice has not yet been described in monolingual contexts, the bilingual practice will be approached in a manner which is recognisable enough to be replicable to a similar monolingual practice.

The above ideas, introduced and developed in the early chapters of the book, were illustrated in the later chapters by means of three case studies. Chapter 4 examined a practice frequently mentioned in the literature on language alternation, namely CS in speech representation. The chapter began by noting that, although the practice has been frequently mentioned in the literature, no systematic account of how it actually works was yet available. That is, given the many sightings of CS in speech representation, the chapter raised additional questions, notably those of how language choice interacts with speech representation. On the other hand, it was also noted that, as an interactional practice, speech representation has been widely investigated in monolingual discourse. In this chapter, one particular explanation of speech representation, known as the demonstration theory, was picked up and used as a hypothesis in order to address the issue of language choice. When this theory was applied to language choice issues, a clear picture of the role of language choice in speech representation emerged. CS occurs in speech representation either because language choice itself is the depictive element or because it is a supportive element. Conversely, therefore, the strength of the demonstration theory was confirmed, as it was shown to account for speech representation in monolingual as well as in bilingual interactions.

Like Chapter 4, Chapter 5 focused on a practice which has been frequently reported in studies of CS, namely CS in repair sequences in bilingual conversation. As in the previous case, the absence of a systematic account of language choice in repair sequences was noted. Again, as in the previous case, it was noted that the practice of conversational repair has been widely investigated in monolingual conversation. Therefore, in the chapter, I drew on existing knowledge about the organisation of repair in conversation and developed an understanding of language choice which is consistent with that previous knowledge. More concretely, I have been able to demonstrate that, in bilingual conversation, language choice is involved in repair sequences either as itself the focus of repair or as an additional resource in the organisation of repair. In turn, this new understanding adds to existing knowledge about conversational repair, especially at the level of the first dimension, as it confirms the foundational claim that any significant aspect of talk organisation can be an object of repair (Schegloff et al., 1977).

Finally, Chapter 6 investigated a practice I referred to as *translinguistic apposition*. A number of significant differences between this practice and the other two can be pointed out. First of all, unlike the other two, the practice has not been mentioned in any previous literature. Secondly, unlike the other two, translinguistic apposition was observed in written texts, more specifically in texts Sebba (2002, 2013) describes as 'most highly regulated'. Thirdly, while both speech representation and repair refer to general interactional phenomena, translinguistic apposition appears to be community-specific. However, despite these differences, the same kinds of question were raised – namely, how the practice works, a similar methodology was used and an account was proposed. As I have indicated in the chapter in question, the issue translinguistic apposition raises is that of its possibility, especially given the Rwandan sociolinguistic context. A generally inductive methodology was used to account for its possibility at the theoretical level and a context-sensitive interpretation was provided, given the context-specificity of the practice.

To summarise, this book has identified an issue with which the study of bilingualism, and of bilingual language use in particular, is faced: namely, that of its continued relevance. It has suggested a way forward: that is, to view bilingualism as consisting of diverse interactional practices and to aim to accumulate an empirically based understanding of those practices. The key question, in each case, will be: how does this particular practice involving the use of two or more languages work? In exploring the answer to this question, the attitude will be to approach data inductively and to mainstream the study of bilingualism. Three case studies illustrating how this programme can be implemented have been proposed. In concluding, an invitation is extended to the bilingualism research community to take forward this programme of study. As I have said in the introductory chapter, I have chosen the 'text as colony' (Hoey, 2001) format for this book precisely because it lends itself to this open invitation.

References

Alfonzetti, Giovanna (1998). The conversational dimension in code-switching between Italian and dialect in Sicily. In P. Auer (ed.). *Code-switching in Conversation: Language, Interaction and Identity.* London: Routledge, 180–211.

Alvarez-Caccamo, Celso (1998). From 'switching code' to 'code-switching': Towards a reconceptualization of communicative codes. In P. Auer (ed.). *Code-switching in Conversation: Language, Interaction and Identity.* London: Routledge, 29–48.

Antaki, Charles and Widdicombe, Sue (1998). Identity as an achievement and as a tool. In C. Antaki and S. Widdicombe. *Identities in Talk.* Cambridge: Cambridge University Press, 1–14.

Auer, Peter (1984). *Bilingual Conversation.* Amsterdam: Benjamins.

Auer, Peter (1988). A conversation analytic approach to code-switching and transfer. In M. Heller (ed.). *Codeswitching.* Berlin: Mouton de Gruyter, 187–214. (Reprint in Li Wei (2000). *The Bilingualism Reader.* London: Routledge, 166–87.)

Auer, Peter (1995). The pragmatics of code-switching: A sequential approach. In L. Milroy and P. Muysken (eds). *One Speaker, Two Languages.* Cambridge: Cambridge University Press, 115–35.

Auer, Peter (1998). Introduction: *Bilingual Conversation* revisited. In P. Auer (ed.). *Code-switching in Conversation.* London: Routledge, 1–24.

Baker, Colin and Prys Jones, Silvia (1998). *Encyclopaedia of Bilingualism and Bilingual Education.* Clevedon: Multilingual Matters.

Baynham, Mike (1996). Direct speech: What is it doing in non-narrative discourse? *Journal of Pragmatics,* 25, 61–81.

Brown, Gillian and Yule, George (1983). *Discourse Analysis.* Cambridge: Cambridge University Press.

Blom, Jan-Petter and Gumperz, John (1972). Social meaning in linguistic structure: Code-switching in Norway. In J. Gumperz and D. Hymes (eds). *Directions in Sociolinguistics.* New York: Holt, Rinehart & Winston, 407–34. (Reprint in Li Wei (ed.) (2000). *The Bilingualism Reader.* London: Routledge, 11–136.)

Boddy, F. A. (1975). General practice medicine. In J. H. Barber and F. A. Boddy (eds). *General Practice Medicine.* Edinburgh: Longman, 1–25.

Bonacina-Pugh, Florence (2012). Researching 'practiced language policies': Insights from Conversation Analysis. *Language Policy*, 11, 213–34.

Button, Graham and Casey, Neil (1984). Generating a topic: The use of topic initial elicitors. In J. M. Atkinson and J. Heritage (eds). *Structures of Social Action*. Cambridge: Cambridge University Press, 167–90.

Byrne, Patrick S. and Long, Barrie E. L. (1976). *Doctors Talking to Patients*. London: HMSO.

Cameron, Deborah (1990). Demythologizing sociolinguistics: Why language does not reflect society. In J. Joseph and T. J. Taylor (eds). *Ideologies of Language*. London: Routledge, 79–93.

Cameron, Deborah (2001). *Working with Spoken Discourse*. London: Sage.

Cashman, Holly R. (2005). Identities at play: Language preference and group membership in bilingual talk in interaction. *Journal of Pragmatics*, 37, 301–15.

Cavalli, Marisa, Coste, Daniel, Crişan, Alexandru and van de Ven, Piet-Hein (2009). *Plurilingual and Intercultural Education as a Project*. Council of Europe Language Policy Division, <http://www.coe.int/t/dg4/linguistic/Source/LE_texts_Source/EducPlurInter-Projet_en.pdf> (last accessed 18 May 2016).

Chan, Brian (2004). Beyond 'contextualization': Code-switching as a 'textualization cue'. *Journal of Language and Social Psychology*, 23, 7–27.

Chin, N. G. Bee and Wigglesworth, Gillian (2007). *Bilingualism: An Advanced Resource Book*. London: Routledge.

Clark, Herbert H. and Gerrig, Richard J. (1990). Quotations as demonstrations. *Language*, 66, 764–805.

Clayman, Steven and Heritage, John (2002). *The News Interview*. Cambridge: Cambridge University Press.

Clift, Rebecca and Holt, Elizabeth (2007). Introduction. In E. Hold and R. Clift (eds). *Reporting Talk: Reported Speech in Interaction*. Cambridge: Cambridge University Press, 1–15.

Constitution of the Republic of Rwanda (2003). *Official Gazette of the Republic of Rwanda*, December 2003 (Special issue).

Coupland, Justine (ed.) (2000). *Small Talk*. Harlow: Pearson Education.

Crawford, James (1992). *Language Loyalties: A Sourcebook on the Official English Controversy*. Chicago: University of Chicago Press.

Drew, Paul (1997). 'Open' class repair initiators in response to sequential sources of troubles in conversation. *Journal of Pragmatics*, 28, 69–101.

Drew, Paul (2003). Comparative analysis of talk-in-interaction in different institutional settings: A sketch. In P. J. Glenn, C. D. Leban and J. Mandelbaum (eds). *Studies in Language and Social Interaction*. Mahwah, NJ: Laurence Erlbaum Associates, 293–308.

Drew, Paul and Heritage, John (1992). Analysing talk at work: An introduction. In P. Drew and J. Heritage (eds). *Talk at Work: Interaction in Institutional Settings*. Cambridge: Cambridge University Press, 3–65.

Drew, Paul and Sorjen, Marja-Leena (1997). Institutional dialogue. In T. A. van Dijk (ed.). *Discourse as Social Interaction*. London: Sage, 92–118.

Eastman, Carol and Stein, Roberta (1993). Language display: Authenticating claims to social identity. *Journal of Multilingual and Multicultural Development*, 14, 187–202.

Fasold, Ralph (1984). *The Sociolinguistics of Society*. Oxford: Blackwell.

Fasold, Ralph (1990). *Sociolinguistics of Language*. Oxford: Blackwell.

Ferguson, Charles (1959). Diglossia. *Word*, 15: 325–40.

Fishman, Joshua (1967). Bilingualism with and without diglossia; diglossia with and without bilingualism. *Journal of Social Issues*, 23, 29–38. (Reprint in L. Wei (ed.) (2000). *The Bilingualism Reader*. London: Routledge, 81–8.)

Fishman, Joshua, Couper, Robert and Newman, Roxana (1971). *Bilingualism in the Barrio*. The Hague: Mouton.

Gafaranga, Joseph (1998). Elements of order in bilingual talk: Kinyarwanda–French language alternation. Unpublished PhD thesis, Lancaster University.

Gafaranga, Joseph (1999). Language choice as a significant aspect of talk organisation: The orderliness of language alternation. *TEXT*, 19, 201–26.

Gafaranga, Joseph (2000). Medium repair versus other-language repair: Telling the medium of a bilingual conversation. *International Journal of Bilingualism*, 33, 1901–25.

Gafaranga, Joseph (2001). Linguistic identities in talk-in-interaction: Order in bilingual conversation. *Journal of Pragmatics*, 33: 1901–25.

Gafaranga, Joseph (2005). Demythologising language alternation studies: Conversational structure versus social structure in bilingual interaction. *Journal of Pragmatics*, 37: 281–300.

Gafaranga, Joseph (2007a). Code-switching as a conversational strategy. In P. Auer and L. Wei (eds). *Handbook of Multilingualism and Multilingual Communication*. Berlin: Mouton de Gruyter, 279–313.

Gafaranga, Joseph (2007b). *Talk in Two Languages*. New York: Palgrave Macmillan.

Gafaranga, Joseph (2009). The conversation analytic model of code-switching. In B. E. Bullock and A. J. Toribio (eds). *The Cambridge Handbook of Linguistic Code-Switching*. Cambridge: Cambridge University Press, 114–26.

Gafaranga, Joseph (2010). Medium request: Talking language shift into being. *Language in Society*, 39, 241–70.

Gafaranga, Joseph (2011). Transition space medium repair: Language shift talked into being. *Journal of Pragmatics*, 42, 118–35.

Gafaranga, Joseph (2012). Language alternation and conversational repair in bilingual conversation. *International Journal of Bilingualism*, 16, 501–27.

Gafaranga, Joseph (2015). Translinguistic apposition in a multilingual media blog in Rwanda: Towards an interpretive perspective in language policy research. *Language in Society*, 44, 87–112.

Gafaranga, Joseph and Britten, Nicky (2003). 'Fire away': The opening sequence in general practice consultations. *Family Practice*, 20, 242–7.

Gafaranga, Joseph and Britten, Nicky (2004). Formulation in general practice consultations. *TEXT*, 24, 147–70.

Gafaranga, Joseph and Britten, Nicky (2005). Talking an institution into being:

The opening sequence in general practice consultations. In K. Richards and P. Seedhouse (eds). *Applying Conversation Analysis*. New York: Palgrave Macmillan, 75–90.

Gafaranga, Joseph, Niyomugabo, Cyprien and Uwizeyimana, Valentin (2013). Micro declared language policy or not? Language-policy-like statements in the rules of procedure of the Rwandan Parliament. *Language Policy*, 12, 313–32.

Gafaranga, Joseph and Torras, Maria-Carme (2001). Language versus medium in the study of bilingual conversation. *International Journal of Bilingualism*, 5, 195–219.

Gal, Susan (1979). *Language Shift: Social Determinants of Language Change in Bilingual Austria*. New York: Academic Press.

García, Ofelia (2009). *Bilingual Education in the 21st Century*. Chichester: Wiley–Blackwell.

Gardner-Chloros, Penelope (2009). *Code-switching*. Cambridge: Cambridge University Press.

Gardner-Chloros, Penelope, Charles, Reeva and Cheshire, Jenny (2000). Parallel patterns? A comparison of monolingual speech and bilingual codeswitching discourse. *Journal of Pragmatics*, 32, 1305–41.

Garfinkel, Harold (1967). *Studies in Ethnomethodology*. Englewood Cliffs, NJ: Prentice Hall.

Garfinkel, Harold and Sacks, Harvey (1970). On formal structures of practical social action. In J. C. McKinney and E. A. Teryakian (eds). *Theoretical Sociology*. New York: Appleton Century Croft, 338–66.

Gasana, Anastase (1984). Bilingualisme et traduction: Le cas du kinyarwanda et du français. *Mineprisec* (vol. and page numbers not recorded).

Goffman, Erving (1967). *Interaction Ritual: Essays on Face-to-face Behaviour*. New York: Doubleday.

Goffman, Erving (1974). *Frame Analysis: An Essay on the Organization of Experience*. Boston: Northeastern University Press.

Goffman, Erving (1981). *Forms of Talk*. Oxford: Blackwell.

Goodwin, Charles and Duranti, Alexandre (1992). Rethinking context: An introduction. In A. Duranti and C. Goodwin (eds). *Rethinking Context*. Cambridge: Cambridge University Press, 1–42.

Green, Steven L. (2002). Rational choice theory: An overview, <business baylor edu/steve_green/green1.doc> (last accessed 15 February 2012).

Gumperz, John (1972). Sociolinguistics and communication in small groups. In J. B. Pride and Janet Holmes (eds). *Sociolinguistics*. Harmondsworth, Middlesex: Penguin Education, 203–24.

Gumperz, John (1981). The linguistic bases of communicative competence. In D. Tannen (ed.). *Analysing Discourse: Text and Talk*. Washington, DC: Georgetown University Press, 324–34.

Gumperz, John (1982). *Discourse Strategies*. Cambridge: Cambridge University Press.

Haakana, Markku (2001). Laughter as a patient's resource: Dealing with delicate aspects of medical interaction. *Text and Talk*, 21, 187–220.

Haakana, Markku (2007). Reported thought in complaint stories. In E. Holt and R. Clift (eds). *Reporting Talk: Reported Speech in Interaction.* Cambridge: Cambridge University Press, 150–79.

Heap, James (1990). Applied ethnomethodology: Looking for the local rationality of reading activities. *Human Studies*, 13, 39–72.

Heath, Christian (1981). The opening sequence in doctor–patient interaction. In P. Atkinson and C. Heath (eds). *Medical Work: Realities and Routines.* Aldershot: Gower, 71–90.

Heath, C. (2002). Demonstrative suffering: The gestural (re)embodiment of symptoms. *Journal of Communication*, 52, 597–616.

Heritage, John (1984). *Garfinkel and Ethnomethodology.* Cambridge: Polity Press.

Heritage, John (1985). Analyzing news interviews: Aspects of the production of talk for an overhearing audience. In T. A. van Dijk (ed.). *Handbook of Discourse Analysis* (vol. 3). London: Academic Press, 95–117.

Heritage, John (1997). Conversation analysis and institutional talk. In D. Silverman (ed.). *Qualitative Research: Theory, Method and Practice.* London: Sage, 161–82.

Heritage, John and Clayman, Steven (2010). *Talk in Action: Interactions, Identities and Institutions.* Chichester: Wiley–Blackwell.

Heritage, John and Greatbatch, David (1991). On the institutional character of institutional talk: The case of news interviews. In D. Boden and D. H. Zimmerman (eds). *Talk and Social Structure.* Cambridge: Polity Press, 93–137.

Heritage, John and Robinson, Jeffrey (2006). Accounting for the visit: Giving reasons for seeking medical care. In J. Heritage and W. Maynard (eds). *Communication in Medical Care: Interaction between Primary Care Physicians and Patients.* Cambridge: Cambridge University Press, 48–85.

Heritage, John and Sefi, Sue (1992). Dilemma of advice: Aspects of the delivery and reception of advice in interactions between health visitors and first-time mothers. In P. Drew and J. Heritage (eds). *Talk at Work.* Cambridge: Cambridge University Press, 359–417.

Heritage, John and Watson, Rob (1979). Formulations as conversational objects. In G. Psathas (ed.). *Everyday Language: Studies in Ethnomethodology.* New York: Ervington, 123–62.

Hoey, Michael (2001). *Textual Interaction: An Introduction to Written Discourse Analysis.* London: Routledge.

Holt, Elizabeth (1996). Reporting on talk: The use of direct reported speech in conversation. *Research on Language and Social Interaction*, 29, 219–45.

Holt, Elizabeth (2007). 'I'm eyeing your chop up mind': Reporting and enacting. In E. Holt and R. Cliff (eds). *Reporting Talk: Reported Speech in Interaction.* Cambridge: Cambridge University Press, 47–80.

Hymes, Dell (1972). On communicative competence. In J. B. Pride and Janet Holmes (eds). *Sociolinguistics.* Harmondsworth, Middlesex: Penguin Education, 33–51.

Ihemere, Kelechukwu (2007). *A Tri-generational Study of Language Choice and Language Shift in Port Harcourt*. Boca Raton, FL: Universal.

Itorero ry'igihugu, Kigali, 2009.

Jefferson, Gail (1979). A technique for inviting laughter and its subsequent acceptance. In G. Psathas (ed.). *Everyday Language: Studies in Ethnomethodology*. New York: Irvington, 79–95.

Jefferson, Gail (1987). Exposed and embedded corrections. In G. Button and J. R. E. Lee (eds). *Talk and Social Organization*. Clevedon: Multilingual Matters, 86–100.

Jørgensen, J. Norman (2008). Polylingual languaging around and among children and adolescents. *International Journal of Multilingualism*, 5, 161–76.

Kasper, Gabriele (2009). Categories, context and comparison in conversation analysis. In H. T. Nguyen and G. Kasper (eds). *Talk in Interaction: Multilingual Perspectives*. Honolulu: Foreign Language Resource Centre, University of Hawai at Mānoa, 1–28.

Kendon, Adam and Ferber, Andrew (1973). A description of some human greetings. In R. P. Michael and J. H. Crook (eds). *Comparative Ecology and Behaviour of Primates*. London: Academic Press, 591–668.

Labov, William (1966). *The Social Stratification of English in New York City*. Washington, DC: Centre for Applied Linguistics.

Laurie, S. S. (1890). *Lectures on Language and Linguistic Method in School*. Cambridge: Cambridge University Press.

Levinson, Stephen (1983). *Pragmatics*. Cambridge: Cambridge University Press.

Liddicoat, Anthony J. (2007). *An Introduction to Conversation Analysis*. London: Continuum.

Marten, Lutz and Kula, Nancy C. (2008). Zambia: 'one Zambia, one nation, many languages'. In A. Simpson (ed.). *Language and National Identity in Africa*. Oxford: Oxford University Press, 291–313.

Meeuwis, Michael and Blommaert, Jan (1998). A monolectal view of code-switching: Layered code-switching among Zairians in Belgium. In P. Auer (ed.). *Code-switching in Conversation*. London: Routledge, 76–98.

Mey, Jacob L. (1993). *Pragmatics: An Introduction*. Oxford: Blackwell.

Milroy, Leslie (1980). *Language and Social Networks*. Oxford: Basil Blackwell.

Milroy, Leslie and Wei, Li (1995). A social network approach to code-switching: The example of a bilingual community in Britain. In L. Milroy and P. Muysken (eds). *One Speaker, Two Languages*. Cambridge: Cambridge University Press, 136–257.

Mkilifi, Abdulaziz (1978). Triglossia and Swahili–English bilingualism in Tanzania. In J. Fishman (ed.). *Advances in the Study of Societal Multilingualism*. The Hague: Mouton, 129–52.

Montvalon, J. B. (2015). Nouvel Obstacle à la ratification de la charte des langues régionales. *Le Monde*, 1 August 2015.

Muysken, Pieter (2000). *Bilingual Speech: A Typology of Code-Mixing*. Cambridge: Cambridge University Press.

Myers, Greg (1991). Functions of reported speech in group discussions. *Applied Linguistics*, 20, 376–401.

Myers-Scotton, Carol (1993a). *Duelling Languages: Grammatical Structure in Codeswitching.* Oxford: Clarendon Press.

Myers-Scotton, Carol (1993b). *Social Motivations for Codeswitching: Evidence from Africa.* Oxford: Clarendon Press.

Myers-Scotton, Carol (1997). Code-switching. In C. Florian (ed.). *Handbook of Sociolinguistics.* Oxford: Blackwell, 217–38.

Myers-Scotton, Carol (1988). Code-switching as indexical of social negotiations. In M. Heller (ed.). *Codeswitching.* Berlin: Mouton de Gruyter, 151–86. (Reprint in L. Wei (ed.) (2000). *The Bilingualism Reader.* London: Routledge, 137–65.)

Myers-Scotton, C. (1999). Explaining the role of norms and rationality in codeswitching. *Journal of Pragmatics*, 32, 1259–71.

Myers-Scotton, Carol (2002). *Contact Linguistics: Bilingual Encounters and Grammatical Outcomes.* Oxford: Oxford University Press.

Myers-Scotton, Carol and Bolonyai, Agnes (2001). Calculating speakers: Codeswitching as a rational choice model. *Language in Society*, 30, 1–28.

Namba, Ayako (2011). Listenership in Japanese interaction: The contribution of laughter. Unpublished PhD dissertation, University of Edinburgh.

Neighbour, Roger (1987). *The Inner Consultation: How to Develop an Effective and Intuitive Consulting Style.* Lancaster: MIT Press.

Otsuji, Emi and Pennycook, Alastair (2009). Metrolingualism: Fixity, fluidity and language in flux. *International Journal of Multilingualism*, 7, 240–54.

Papageorgiou, Ifigenia (2012). When language policy and pedagogy conflict: Pupils' and educators' 'practiced language policies' in an English-medium kindergarten classroom in Greece. Unpublished PhD dissertation, University of Edinburgh.

Pendleton, David, Schofield, Theo, Tate, Peter and Havelock, Peter (1984). *The Consultation: An Approach to Learning and Teaching.* Oxford: Oxford University Press.

Pendleton, David, Schofield, Theo, Tate, Peter and Havelock, Peter (2003). *The New Consultation.* Oxford: Oxford University Press.

Pike, Kenneth L. (1967). *Language in Relation to a Unified Theory of the Structure of Human Behavior.* The Hague: Mouton.

Pomerantz, Anita and Fehr, B. J. (1997). Conversation analysis: An approach to the study of social action as sense making practices. In T. A. van Dijk (ed.). *Discourse as Social Interaction.* London: Sage, 64–91.

Poplack, Shana (1980). 'Sometimes I'll start a sentence in Spanish *y termino en español*': Towards a typology and code-switching. *Linguistics*, 18, 581–618. (Reprint in L. Wei (ed.) (2000). *The Bilingualism Reader.* London: Routledge, 221–56.)

Pridham, Francesca (2001). *The Language of Conversation.* London: Routledge.

Psathas, George (1995). *Conversation Analysis: The Study of Talk-in-interaction.* London: Sage.

Quirk, Randolph, Greenbaum, Sidney, Leech, Geoffrey and Svartvik, Jan (1985). *A Comprehensive Grammar of the English Language*. London: Longman.

Rae, John and Kerby, Joanne (2007). Designing context for reporting tactical talk. In E. Holt and R. Clift (eds). *Reporting Talk: Reported Speech in Interaction*. Cambridge: Cambridge University Press, 179–94.

Ricento, Thomas (2000). Historical and theoretical perspectives in language policy and planning. In T. Recento (ed.). *Ideology, Politics and Language Policies*. Amsterdam: John Benjamins, 9–24.

Richards, Keith (2005). Introduction. In K. Richards and P. Seedhouse (eds). *Applying Conversation Analysis*. New York: Palgrave Macmillan, 1–18.

Robinson, Jeffrey D. (2006). Soliciting patients' presenting concerns. In J. Heritage and W. Maynard (eds). *Communication in Medical Care: Interaction between Primary Care Physicians and Patients*. Cambridge: Cambridge University Press, 22–47.

Rubio-Marin, Ruth (2003). Language rights: Exploring competing rationales. In W. Kymlicka and A. Patten (eds). *Language Rights and Political Theory*. Oxford: Oxford University Press, 52–79.

Ruusuvuori, Johanna (2000). Control in the medical consultation: Giving and receiving the reason for the visit in Finnish primary care encounters. *Acto Universitatis Temperensis*, 16, <http:acta.fi./pdf/951-44-4755-7.pdf> (last accessed 18 May 2016).

Ruusuvuori, Johanna (2005). Comparing homoeopathic and general practice consultations: The case of problem presentation. *Communication & Medicine*, 2, 123–36.

Saadah, Eman (2009). The 'how are you' sequence in telephone openings in Arabic. *Studies in the Linguistic Sciences: Illinois Working Papers*, 171–89.

Sacks, Harvey (1975). Everyone has to lie. In M. Sanches and B. G. Blount (eds). *Sociocultural Dimension of Language Use*. New York: Academic Press, 57–80.

Sacks, Harvey, Schegloff, Emanuel and Jefferson, Gail (1974). A simplest systematics for the organization of turn taking for conversation. In J. Schenkein (ed.). *Studies in the Organization of Conversational Interaction*. New York: Academic Press, 7–55.

Samuelson, Beth L. and Freedman, Sarah W. (2010). Language policy, multilingual education and power in Rwanda. *Language Policy*, 9, 191–215.

Saussure, Ferdinand de (1959). *Course in General Linguistics*. New York: McGraw–Hill.

Schegloff, Emanuel (1968). Sequencing in conversational openings. *American Anthropologist*, 70, 1075–95.

Schegloff, Emanuel (1986). The routine as achievement. *Human Studies*, 9, 111–51.

Schegloff, Emanuel (1992). On talk and its institutional occasions. In P. Drew and J. Heritage (eds). *Talk at Work*. Cambridge: Cambridge University Press, 101–36.

Schegloff, Emanuel (2000). When 'others' initiate repair. *Applied Linguistics*, 21, 205–43.

Schegloff, Emanuel (2007). *Sequencing in Conversation: A Primer in Conversation Analysis* (vol. 1). Cambridge: Cambridge University Press.

Schegloff, Emanuel, Jefferson, Gail and Sacks, Harvey (1977). The preference for self-correction in the organization of repair in conversation. *Language*, 53, 361–82.

Schegloff, Emanuel and Sacks, Harvey (1973). Opening up closings. *Semiotica*, 8, 289–327. (Reprint in R. Turner (ed.) (1974). *Ethnomethodology: Selected Readings*. Harmondsworth: Penguin Education, 233–64.)

Schenkein, Jim (1978). A sketch of an analytic mentality for the study of conversational interaction. In J. Schenkein (ed.). *Studies in the Organization of Conversational Interaction*. New York: Academic Press, 1–6.

Scott, John (2000). Rational choice theory. In G. Browning, A. Halcli and F. Webster (eds). *Understanding Contemporary Society: Theories of the Present*. London: Sage, 126–38.

Scotton, Carol (1983). Negotiation of identities in conversation: A theory of markedness and codeswitching. *International Journal of the Sociology of Language*, 44: 115–36.

Scotton, Carol (1988). Codeswitching as indexical of social negotiation. In M. Heller (ed.). *Codeswitching*. Berlin: Mouton de Gruyter, 151–86. (Reprint in L. Wei (ed.) (2000). *The Bilingualism Reader*. London: Routledge, 137–65.)

Searle, John (1969). *Speech Acts*. Cambridge: Cambridge University Press.

Sebba, Mark (1998). A congruence approach to the syntax code-switching. *International Journal of Bilingualism*, 2, 1–20.

Sebba, Mark (2002). Regulated spaces: language alternation in writing, <www. ling.lancs.ac.uk/staff/mark/vigo/regspace> (last accessed 19 March 2013).

Sebba, Mark (2013). Multilingualism in written discourse: An approach to the analysis of multilingual texts. *International Journal of Bilingualism*, 17, 97–118.

Sebba, Mark and Wootton, Tony (1998). We, they and identity: Sequential versus identity-related explanation in code-switching. In P. Auer (ed.). *Code-switching in Conversation*. London: Routledge, 262–86.

Shin, Sarah J. and Milroy, Lesley (2000). Conversational code-switching among Korean–English bilingual children. *International Journal of Bilingualism*, 4, 351–84.

Shohamy, Elena G. (2006). *Language Policy*. London: Routledge.

Sidnell, Jack (2010). *Conversation Analysis*. Chichester: Wiley–Blackwell.

Sidnell, Jack (2014). Basic conversation analytic methods. In T. Stivers and J. Sidnell (eds). *Handbook of Conversation Analysis*. West Sussex: Wiley Blackwell, 77–99.

Silverman, Jonathan, Kurtz, Suzanne and Draper, Juliet (2005). *Skills for Communicating with Patients* (2nd edn). Oxford: Radcliffe.

Sinclair, A. (1976). The sociolinguistic significance of the form of requests used in service encounters. Unpublished diploma dissertation, University of Cambridge.

Spolsky, Bernard (2004). *Language Policy*. Cambridge: Cambridge University Press.

Stevenson, Fiona, Britten, Nicky, Barber, Nick, Barry, Christine A. and Bradley, Colin P. (2000). Research note: Qualitative methods and prescribing research. *Journal of Clinical Pharmacy and Therapeutics*, 25, 317–24.

Tannen, Deborah (1989). *Talking Voices: Repetition, Dialogue and Imagery in Conversational Discourse.* Cambridge: Cambridge University Press.

Ten Have, Paul (1999). *Doing Conversation Analysis: A Practical Guide.* London: Sage.

Thompson, Darren and Ciechanowski, Paul S. (2003). Attaching a new meaning to the patient–physician relationship in family practice. *Journal of the American Board of Family Practice*, 16, 219–26.

Thompson, Geoff (1996). Voices in the text: Discourse perspectives on language reports. *Applied Linguistics*, 17, 501–30.

Torras, Maria-Carme (1999). Selection of medium in conversation: A study of trilingual service encounters. Unpublished MA thesis, Universitat Autònoma de Barcelona.

Torras, Maria-Carme (2005). Social identity and language choice in bilingual service talk. In K. Richards and P. Seedhouse (eds). *Applying Conversation Analysis.* New York: Palgrave Macmillan, 107–23.

Torras, Maria-Carme and Gafaranga, Joseph (2002). Social identities and language alternation in non-formal institutional bilingual talk: Trilingual service encounters in Barcelona. *Language in Society*, 31, 527–49.

Vinkhuyzen, Erik and Szymanski, Margaret H. (2005). Would you like to do it yourself? Service requests and their non-granting responses. In K. Richards and P. Seedhouse (eds). *Applying Conversation Analysis.* Basingstoke: Palgrave Macmillan, 91–106.

Wei, Li (1994). *Three Generations, Two Languages, One Family: Language Choice and Language Shift in a Chinese Community in Britain.* Clevedon: Multilingual Matters.

Wei, Li (1998). The 'why' and 'how' questions in the analysis of conversational code-switching. In P. Auer (ed.). *Code-switching in Conversation.* London: Routledge, 156–76.

Wei, Li (2000). Dimensions of bilingualism. In L. Wei. *The Bilingualism Reader.* London: Routledge, 3–25.

Wei, Li (2002). 'What do you want me to say?' On the conversation analysis approach to bilingual interaction. *Language in Society*, 31, 159–80.

Whalen, Marilyn M. and Zimmerman, Don H. (1987). Sequential and institutional contexts in calls for help. *Social Psychology Quarterly*, 50, 172–85.

Zimmerman, Don H. (1992). The interactional organization of calls for emergency assistance. In P. Drew and J. Heritage (eds). *Talk at Work.* Cambridge: Cambridge University Press, 418–69.

Index

other-language repair, 114–15
other-repair, 101–12, 116
ratification of repair, 112–13
repairable class, 8, 97–100, 104, 106,
    111, 113, 114–16
repairers, 107–12
repair initiators, 30–1, 98, 101–7,
    114–15
same turn repairs, 107–8
second position repairs, 109–12
self-initiated medium self-repair, 133
self-initiated other-repair problem, 37,
    109, 114–15, 134
self-initiation of repair, 101–7
self-repair, 95, 101, 107–12, 116
sequential analysis, 9, 112
third position repairs, 34, 107, 109,
    112–13
transition space repair, 34, 36, 107,
    108–9, 136
repetition, as repair practice, 102, 103,
    105–6, 112, 113
reported speech *see* direct speech
    reporting (DSR)
restrictive appositives, 117
rewards versus costs in interactions, 23–4
Ricento, Thomas, 143
Richards, Keith, 8
rights and obligations, 23, 25–8
Robinson, Jeffrey D., 46, 47, 48, 58, 59, 64,
    66, 69
Roosevelt, President Theodore, 2
Rubio-Marin, Ruth, 137
Russian, 124
Rwanda
    Constitution of the Republic of
        Rwanda, 123, 137–8, 140, 141
    direct speech reporting, 74
    macro policies, 137–42
    multilingualism, 2–3, 119, 123, 137–42
    official languages, 119, 123, 137–42
    schools and education, 123–4, 141
Rwandisme, 3
'Rwandophone' category, lack of, 123

Saadah, Eman, 53
Sacks, Harvey, 36, 37, 51, 100
same action-type sequence series, 52–3,
    65
same turn repair, 107–8
Saussure, Ferdinand de, 15
Schegloff, Emanuel, 8, 34, 45, 47, 48, 50,
    51, 52, 53, 54, 55, 60, 61, 63, 97, 100,
    101, 102, 103, 114, 115, 136
Schenkein, Jim, 8

scholarship, 4
schools and education, 123–4, 141
scripts, 25–6; *see also* conventionalised
    exchanges
Searle, John, 22, 98
Sebba, Mark, 9, 19, 31, 43, 117, 119,
    124–6, 127, 131, 132, 148
second attempts, 34
second pair parts, 34, 37, 51–5, 64–5,
    105–6, 110–11
second position repair, 109–12
Sefi, Sue, 98
selection of next speaker, 37
self-initiated medium self-repair, 133
self-initiated other-repair problem, 37,
    109, 114–15, 134
self-initiation of repair, 101–7
self-repair, 95, 101, 107–12, 116
semantics
    inherent meaning potential, 19
    interactional negotiation for meaning,
        132
    meaningful discourse cues, 15
    semantic value of code-switching
        (CS), 16–17
sequence organisation
    adjacency pairs, 34, 37, 51–5, 64–5, 100,
        105, 106
    sequence expansion, 52
sequential analysis
    howareyou sequence, 61–3, 70–1
    inductive perspective, 8–9
    repair practices, 9, 112
    talk organisation, 33–5
    translinguistic apposition, 132
serious actions (versus non-serious), 79,
    80
service requests, 55–6
Shohamy, Elena G., 137, 140
Sidnell, Jack, 41, 101, 116
signalling functions, 95, 113, 116
signs, 78
Silverman, Jonathan, 46, 58, 63
simultaneity, 112
situational versus metaphorical code-
    switching, 16–17
sociability, 46, 51, 55–6, 66, 68, 70
social categorisation, 92
social class differentiation, 44–5
social conventions, 19
social distance, creating, 89, 92
Social Exchange Theory, 23
social identity, 132
social indexicality of language varieties,
    28–31